J. E. (James Elgin) Wetherell

Over the Sea

A Summer Trip to Britain

J. E. (James Elgin) Wetherell

Over the Sea
A Summer Trip to Britain

ISBN/EAN: 9783744714587

Printed in Europe, USA, Canada, Australia, Japan

Cover: Foto ©Andreas Hilbeck / pixelio.de

More available books at **www.hansebooks.com**

OVER THE SEA.

A Summer Trip to Britain.

BY

J. E. WETHERELL.

STRATHROY, ONT.:
PUBLISHED BY EVANS BROTHERS.
1892.

PREFACE.

The twelve sketches in this little book were written over a year ago in serial form for a periodical. They are now republished in this volume without alteration.

The reader will see that the point of view in these sketches is mainly that of a traveller guided by literary and historical attractions. Commerce and politics, the farm and the shop, science and statistics, receive no attention whatever. The writer's journey to the east was a journey to scenes associated with the charms of history and poetry.

The writer is encouraged to believe that this record of his rambles will revive happy memories of the old land in many readers who were born over the sea, and that it will whet the literary appetite of others and excite in them desires to visit the interesting scenes to which his feeble pen has done scanty justice.

STRATHROY, FEB. 27TH, 1892.

CONTENTS.

		PAGE
I.	—The Ocean Voyage	5
II.	—Glasgow and the Land of Burns	15
III.	—The Highland Lakes	22
IV.	—Edinburgh	30
V.	—Melrose and Abbotsford	41
VI.	—London—St. Paul's Cathedral and Westminster Abbey	50
VII.	—London—The Zoological Gardens, Madame Tussaud's, The Crystal Palace, The National Gallery, The British Museum, South Kensington Museum	61
VIII.	—London Life	74
IX.	—Stratford-on-Avon	84
X.	—Oxford and Cambridge	92
XI.	—Tennyson Land—Lincoln, Louth, Mablethorpe	102
XII.	—Tennyson Land—Horncastle and Somersby. Conclusion	111

OVER THE SEA.

I.

THE VOYAGE.

"I never was on the dull, tame shore,
But I loved the great sea more and more.
The sea! the sea! the open sea!
The blue, the fresh, the ever free!"
—BARRY CORNWALL.

It is eight o'clock on the morning of July 10th. The Brooklyn pier of the State-Line Steamship Company is crowded with an excited throng. The good ship "Nevada" is taking on her passengers and their luggage. All is bustle and confusion. The published lists of saloon passengers that are being distributed contain the names of only one hundred and nine persons, but at least two or three hundred others have come down to see the steamer off. Some of these are mere idlers attracted hither by the curiosity of the moment. Some have come to sell their wares to the departing voyagers. But many of them are relatives and friends of those about to launch on the uncertain sea. Eager handshakings and affectionate embraces are soon over. The gangway is hastily taken up. Off moves the ship from *terra firma*. A dialogue of waving handkerchiefs from pier and deck accompanied by oft-shouted "goodbyes" lends animation to the scene of departure, and helps to keep up the flagging spirits of many whose moist eyes tell of emotion repressed. Everyone feels that the die is now cast and that the hazards of the sea must be calmly met. Even the sad faces soon light up with interest and the fainting hearts recover their accustomed resolution.

As we steam out of New York harbor we obtain a fine view of the metropolis of America. As we move away from shore the panorama of the coast is very pleasing and restful to the eye on this clear summer day. Sandy Hook is passed at eleven o'clock. Soon the shore appears only as a blue line fading slowly away from the distant horizon.

A strange sensation of solitariness takes possession of the traveller who leaves his native land for the first time to cross the broad ocean alone, and who, as he paces the deck while the distant hills are just receding from sight, sees no familiar face amid the groups that congregate here and there to take the last peering look at the vanishing continent that contains all that is dearest in life to them and to him. The words of the "Ancient Mariner" start up in the memory with thrilling vividness:

"Alone, alone, all, all alone,
Alone on a wide, wide sea!"

When the exhilarating excitements incident to leaving port are once over, the solitary traveller is at the mercy of all the latent forces of his being that tend to produce depression of spirits. The only safe resource in such straits is the fellowship of an exciting book, or still better, the cheering companionship of living men and women. From the latter the stranger is by no means cut off on board ship. The ocean has a social code of its own. With the last sight of land all the supernumerary conventionalities of town and city, often as stiff and formal as frowning peaks and rugged mountains, are thrown overboard ; and with the ease with which one dons a change of raiment is assumed a style of life and address as free as roving breeze and flowing wave. In twenty-four hours after the lifting of the anchor every passenger who is not rigidly exclusive will have a score of acquaintances, and two or three new friendships will be already in the bud.

There are travellers—and travellers. An ocean voyage is sure to bring one into contact with many amiable and interesting people, but what odd specimens of humanity one also meets ! There is the Chicago merchant who, after the toil and moil of many busy years which have won him a substantial fortune, is going to Europe with his big and clever (?) son, to visit places of which he knows as little as he does of the constellations in the heavens above him. There is the dandy from the same western city whose assiduous efforts at subduing feminine hearts are as ludicrous as they are vain. There is the glum and taciturn preacher from New York who frowns at harmless hilarity and grinds his teeth with fire-and-brimstone vigor at the sight of a game of cards. There is the frisky middle-aged gentleman from Rochester whose constant antics are very diverting and who is the more interesting on account of the accomplishments and attractions of his lovely wife. There is the dyspeptic from the west who, instead of keeping his incurable ailment under cover, is constantly craving and asking for the sympathy of indifferent and disgusted fellow-voyagers. There is the chronic grumbler from New England who hardly opens his lips except to cavil and censure, who finds fault with captain and crew, with food and berth, with wind and weather, and whose only saving quality is an occasional kindly reference to an absent wife and family. There is the old Scotch lady who is crossing the sea with her dog " Bobby," and whose solicitude for the wee quadruped's welfare is as keen as that of any mother on board for the comfort of her helpless child. There, too, is the jolly fat bachelor from Toronto whose genial countenance, affable manners and delightful talk make him the most striking figure on board. He is mentioned in this category not because of his oddity but because he more than anyone else is the " observed of all observers."

Had we a storm at sea ? Not a veritable storm, but for two days we had very rough water. On Friday, July 11th, a stiff breeze sprang up as we entered the Gulf Stream. The deck, which had been a scene of joy and life, soon became a scene of discomfort and distress. Before evening nearly all the passengers had been subdued by Neptune. All that night the ship rolled and pitched incessantly and undisturbed sleep was impossible. A few passengers who at five o'clock next morning fled from the stifling atmosphere of the state-rooms to breathe the fresh air above were driven in by the lashing waves that in their angry fury swept the decks with increasing volume and frequency. Even the hurricane-deck afforded but a precarious refuge to those who were determined to be out in the fresh air. The ship rolled from side to side, reaching at times an incline of nearly forty-five degrees, and as she staggered and plunged it seemed almost miraculous that she recovered her balance. Noon came and still the wind abated not. Nearly all the passengers went without their meals that day. Clattering and breaking dishes and all the attendant discomforts of the saloon were not very appetizing. Rock, rock, rock, went the ship through the long, weary hours. Saturday night was quite as trying as Friday night. The port-holes had not been open for two days and the air was very foul. With Sunday came a blessed change. During the rest of the voyage we had ideal sea weather and everyone's enjoyment was far greater than if we had had a monotony of calm and comfort.

On shipboard the occupations of the passengers are not numerous. When the weather is fine the games of ship-quoits and shuffle-board always have their votaries. The smoking-room is at all hours a centre of attraction for those who like the weed. The antithesis of this is the music-room,—a resort as distinctively feminine as the other is masculine. The deck, in fair weather, is crowded with the great bulk of the passengers,—

some wrapped up and stretched at full length on their sea-chairs,—some lolling over the quarter-railing,—some lying flat in slumber, even at midday, on the clean oaken planks,—some reading light literature by fits and starts,—many promenading the quarter-deck, especially before and after meal-time.. All these amusements and diversions, however, are of an unsettled and desultory nature. Sufficient unto the hour is the employment thereof. " A life on the ocean wave " has no plan, no method, no care, no anxiety, no pressing claims, no engrossing duties. To the majority of sea-travellers each day is filled with vacant nothings, and a vacuous expression soon settles on many faces. There is indeed one sight that rouses the active interest of the most lethargic,—the sight of a distant sail or of the smoke from a passing steamer. There is one sound,—one welcome sound that arrests the attention and controls the movements of everyone, whatever the occupation of the passing moment,—the sound of the bell that invites the hungry passengers to the dining-table below.

The only thing that detracts from the romance of a sea-voyage is—the passengers. The capricious sea will not yield all her secrets and her charms to collective scrutiny. Life on a sailing-ship, alone with the officers and crew and a few kindred spirits, seems to be the ideal sea-life. So much of one's environment on a crowded ocean-steamer is of the earth earthy. There is a suggestion of rushing cars and clashing machinery in the very throb and tremor of the great monster that is hurrying us over the waters :

> "For the throb of the pulse never stops
>   In the heart of the ship,
> As her measures of water and fire
>   She drinks down at a sip."

One must get away to some secluded part of the deck, far from the engines, and far too from all distracting human influences, if he would put himself in touch with the spirits of wave and wind and sky.

What countless creatures teem in the fathomless depths of ocean or sweep over its boundless expanse. There goes the huge whale, heaving his broad back above the tumbling billows. There grins the ravenous shark, darting through the blue waters with a death-menacing motion. There shoals of porpoises leap and sport, trying to equal the speed of the vessel. Yonder fly the beautiful sea-gulls with their weird and plaintive cries. The dullest imagination can pass beyond the presence of the visible and peer into the gulfs below and view the innumerable swarms of monsters that roam the watery valleys.

Many reflections press upon a thoughtful mind in mid-Atlantic. The floor of the abysses below is strewn with fearful wrecks, and whitening bones of mariners whose cries have sounded on this very air. Over this highway of the nations, bound on missions of peace or destined for deeds of war, countless ships have sailed for many centuries. Even now the keel of our vessel may be cutting the track of the ship that changed the course of American history, or that carried our ancestors to the New World.

What an ominous aspect have those life-boats that hang at the sides of the deck ! How suggestive they are of the awful possibility that before the voyage is over we may be floating in them over this solitary waste of waters at the mercy of the fickle elements ! More sternly suggestive still of possible peril are the many life-preservers to be seen in every part of the ship. The winds and waves may be cruel to a struggling boat, but what awful terrors must be those of the unfortunate that is obliged to have final recourse to one of these inflated life belts.

There is a strange magic and mystery about the sea. Ever since the genesis of our world when "the gathering together of the waters called he seas" man has been at the same time terrified by and fascinated by the mighty main. Poets of all ages, who above all men are capable of receiving deep impressions, have sung of the majesty and the beauty of the sea. Among modern poets Byron and Swinburne have felt most powerfully the ocean's charms. Readers of Byron know well with what exultation he always seizes this favorite theme, the culmination of his ardor being reached in the famous stanzas of Childe Harold beginning

"Roll on, thou deep and dark blue ocean—roll !"

Readers of Swinburne know well that it is the beauty rather than the strength of the sea that has engaged his affections. The soft music of summer waves can be heard in those stanzas beginning :

> "Dawn is dim on the dark soft water,
> Soft and passionate, dark and sweet."

A volume might be written about the ocean, yes many volumes, but the length of this chapter is a warning that it is time to get to shore. After a week of perfect weather a day of fog followed as our ship approached the coast of Ireland. The incessant blowing of the dreary fog horn and other attendant discomforts of the fog made us quite eager to see the land.

What a delightful throng of new sensations rush upon a Canadian who for the first time comes in sight of Europe ! What memories and associations crowd up at the mention of that ancient name,—a name connected with the legends of childhood, the tasks of school days, and the more agreeable studies of maturer years.

We sight Innistrahull on the Donegal coast on Monday morning at daylight after eleven days' sailing. After touching at Moville, the port of Londonderry, the ship speeds towards Glasgow. Many pleasant glimpses of green fields and rugged cliffs are obtained as we skirt the north coast of Ireland. The ruins of "Green Castle" give to us travellers from the New World a thrilling introduction to the Old. The sail through the North Channel past the Mull of Cantire, and up the Firth of Clyde past Arran and Bute prepare us by degrees for the

> "Land of brown heath and shaggy wood,
> Land of the mountain and the flood."

The ship reaches Greenock just in time to run up

the river before the ebb of the tide. The principal object of interest to be seen as we move slowly up the river is Dumbarton Castle,—a ruin as old as the Scoto-Saxon monarchy, if not dating back to Roman times. The scenery of the Clyde is very pleasing. On one side of the river are the highlands and lochs and crags crowned with ancient castles, and on the other parks and farms and manor halls. Presently the river becomes little more than a large canal enclosed between the banks of pastoral meadows. As we approach the city we see forests of tall masts and the skeletons of innumerable ships and are not surprised to learn that this Glasgow is perhaps the most famous city in the world for the building of sea-going vessels. We have now reached our port and the birth-place of the sturdy vessel that has carried us safely over three thousand miles of sea.

II.

GLASGOW AND THE LAND OF BURNS.

Glasgow is not only the largest city in Scotland, but it is also the chief seat of manufactures and commerce. It is a city of smoke and turmoil, furnishing but few attractions to the tourist. There are, however, a few places of interest to which at least a flying visit should be paid.

George Square is an extensive open space in the very heart of the great city. It is a place of public monuments, the largest being Sir Walter Scott's column, surmounted by a colossal statue of the great poet and novelist. Other monuments of special interest are those erected in memory of Sir John Moore, Dr. Livingstone, James Watt, and the poets Burns and Campbell. George Square is a much frequented promenade, especially in the evening after the closing of the public buildings of all kinds that face the quadrangle on every side.

Glasgow Cathedral, at the top of High Street, is a very ancient building, dating back exactly three hundred years before the discovery of America. Its modern boast is a display of stained glass more brilliant and more abundant than that of any other edifice in Great Britain. The crypt of the cathedral, long used as a parish church, figures prominently in Scott's "Rob Roy."

A visitor to Glasgow from across the sea whose advent occurs in Exhibition Week will see Old World life in some of its most sinister aspects. If he take a walk up Argyle Street at half-past nine in the evening —the twilight hour in July—he must be prepared to have his sensibilities continually shocked by horrible street brawls and harrowing scenes of poverty and sin. Throngs of drunken men, hundreds of half-clad women hurrying over the stones with bare and bleeding feet, scores of little children even at this late hour of the evening wandering aimlessly or crying in anxious quest,— these are the pitiable creatures that our boasted civilization has failed to civilize,—and that too in a land where religion and education and philanthropy have reached high-water mark. O these clamant social disorders of this nineteenth century! What beneficent angel from the merciful skies will bring the perfect panacea? Must patience have her perfect work in the slow evolution of better things, or is the great world soon to "spin down the ringing grooves of change?"

THE LAND OF BURNS.

July 22nd, 1890, will always be to me a memorable day. Up to that time my knowledge of the homes and haunts of the poets had been obtained entirely from the printed page. On that day I saw face to face many scenes of poetic renown and breathed the very atmosphere that had stirred the strings of Burns's lyre.

OVER THE SEA.

A journey by railway to the town of Ayr carries you through the famous manufacturing town of Paisley and the burgh of Irvine, the birth-place of the poet Montgomery. The rural scenery, when the train has carried you well away from Glasgow, is richly attractive. You see from the window of the railway carriage many fine landscapes diversified by hills and mountains, glens and vales, rushing streams and gently-flowing rivulets.

The town of Ayr stands at the mouth of the river of the same name. Although occupying low ground it commands delightful views of Arran over the Firth of Clyde and of Cunningham up the coast. In the town itself there are many objects of literary interest. The tourist will not neglect the "Twa Brigs" made famous in Burns' humorous dialogue between the "Sprites that owre the Brigs of Ayr preside":

"Ane on the Auld Brig his airy shape uprears,
 The ither flutters o'er the rising piers."

The Wallace Tower on High Street will also claim attention. This structure now contains the "drowsy dungeon clock" mentioned by Burns in the poem just named. Only a few rods distant is "Tam O'Shanter Inn," where Tam and Souter Johnny sitting by the brightly blazing ingle drank too deeply of the gracious landlady's ale. The old inn has an ancient appearance with its roof of primitive thatch and its lower windows protected by antique shutters.

Ayr is a rich and busy town, but it would scarcely be known beyond the limits of Britain were it not for its association with the name of Burns and for the sterling credential which he has given it:

> "Auld Ayr, wham ne'er a town surpasses
> For honest men and bonnie lasses."

A drive of two miles south from Ayr over a perfect road (all Scotch roads are in excellent condition) brings the tourist to the central point of interest,—the "Burns's Cottage," the birthplace of the poet and the very scene of the "Cottar's Saturday Night." It is a long low white building. The older portion, thatch-covered and battered by time, remains nearly as it was in 1759 when Burns first saw the dim light of day through the small windows of this "lowly shed." To inspect the cottage one pays a fee of six pence. On the Saturday preceding my visit eleven hundred persons entered the cottage door. Fortunate would the poor bard have thought himself a hundred years ago if he could have had a small fraction of the interest which the present owners of the cottage are reaping from the principal of his splendid fame.

An indescribable sensation seizes the visitor as he enters the room where Robert Burns was born, and, walking over the cool, broken stone slabs towards the farthest corner, sees in a nook of the wall the very bed where the poet's mother stilled his infant cries. In the same room are the old tall family clock, the dining table and some ancient chairs. There too are the "wee bit ingle" and the "clean hearthstane." There is the door at which the "neibor lad" rapped—a heavy oak door fastened securely by a bolt encrusted by a century's rust and by a crooked iron hook pushed well down into its bulky staple. Many curiosities connected with the poet's career are deposited in an adjoining room. Various pictures of Burns adorn the walls and many of his manuscripts and letters are there exhibited in cases.

O lowly cottage of Scotland's peasant bard! What is it about thee that draws curious travellers from distant continents and the remotest isles of the sea? Day by day through countless years foreign feet will cross thy humble threshold, and noisy voices will be hushed to a whisper, and reverent heads will be uncovered, and careful hands will touch thy sacred contents, and beating hearts will feel thy subtle influence, and soaring spirits will fly away beyond thy narrow bounds to commune with the spirit of him who has given us so many breathing thoughts and burning words. O lowly cottage, may wind and weather spare thee long. The glory of thy ploughboy's genius has touched thy simplicity and turned it into splendor, has touched thy poverty and made it grandly rich.

About half a mile south of Burns's cottage is "Alloway's auld haunted Kirk," the scene of the revel of the fiends in "Tam O' Shanter," the place
" Whare ghaists and houlets nightly cry."
The Kirk is a small, plain, roofless structure. Cut into the mouldy stone is the date 1513, which is presumably the date of erection. The old ruined church is a fit haunt for eighteenth century ghosts. Surrounding the

Kirk is an ancient cemetery where lies the dust of Burns's father and mother. Near Alloway Kirk is the Burns' monument, built in 1820 at a cost of $15000. The interior of the monument contains many interesting relics, among them the very Bible that the poet presented to "Highland Mary" when he plighted his troth to her. In the vicinity of the monument is the river Doon spanned by the "Auld Brig" which figures so prominently in the narrative of Tam O' Shanter's flight from the pursuing witches. From the middle of the bridge one gets a fine view of the luxuriant scenery of the "Banks and Braes O' Bonny Doon." One feels as he looks out over the gorgeous prospect from the vantage-point of this old stone bridge that it would have been a wonder if the fruitful years had not produced a poet in such a rich environment. Only one who has seen this pastoral paradise and has quaffed this mellow air can appreciate the sad, sweet dirge of the lovely lady over the dead affection of her betrayer:

> "Ye banks and braes o' bonny Doon,
> How can ye bloom sae fresh and fair;
> How can ye chant, ye little birds,
> And I sae weary, fu' o' care!"

There are many other places of interest in the "Land of Burns" than those which I have here named, but I mention only those which I had the pleasure of seeing on that peaceful summer day which can never be forgotten. As I returned to Ayr on my way back to Glasgow I recalled the time when poor Burns, oppressed with many cares, meditated a voyage to Jamai-

ca to try his fortunes in the New World. Well for
literature that the steerage-passenger who had paid his
nine guineas never embarked. All readers of Burns
are familiar with his farewell to Ayr and to Scotland.
As I took my farwell of Ayr the last stanza of Burns's
well-known song assumed a new impressiveness :

> " Farewell old Coila's hills and dales,
> Her heathy moors and winding vales ;
> The scenes where wretched fancy roves,
> Pursuing past unhappy loves !
> Farewell, my friends ! farewell, my foes !
> My peace with these, my love with those—
> The bursting tears my heart declare :
> Farewell the bonny banks of Ayr ! "

III.

THE HIGHLAND LAKES.

A more delightful tour for a July day can scarcely be imagined than a journey from Glasgow to Loch Lomond, up the Loch to Inversnaid, through the region of "The Lady of the Lake," and thence, by way of Sterling, to Edinburgh. This trip can be made in one day and for one gold sovereign.

The tourist leaves Glasgow at eight o'clock in the morning, taking the train for Balloch, a town at the foot of Loch Lomond. The railroad runs along the Clyde for fourteen miles, and then, opposite the castled hill of Dumbarton, turns sharply northward and traverses the valley of the river Leven for six miles. On the banks of this river are the villages of Alexandria, Bonhill, and Renton, near the last of which was born in 1721, Tobias Smollett, one of the three great British novelists of the last century. At Balloch a pretty little steamer is waiting to convey up the lake a hundred excursionists, mostly sons and daughters of the soil.

Loch Lomond, "The Queen of the Scottish Lakes," "The Loch of a Hundred Isles," is the largest lake in Great Britain. It is twenty miles long, its width varying from five miles to half-a-mile. Nowhere in the world, surely, can be found scenery more picturesque and romantic. As we steamed away from Balloch pier a vision of majesty and loveliness was gradually unfolded that could not be exaggerated by painter or by poet. We threaded our way amongst innumerable islands crowned with verdure of matchless variety and beauty. As I heard "the accents of the mountain tongue" in the speech of those about me, and saw those blooming northern faces, as I glanced to the ancient hills and mountains that cradled us in on every side, to the myriads of rills that leaped and gushed down grassy slopes and rugged steeps, to the exquisite contour of the coast as satisfying as the plump roundness of childish cheeks, to the limpid waters that rippled to the gentle breeze, to the wreaths of mist that would swoop down upon us as if by magic and then silently and suddenly steal away, as I viewed the gorgeous coloring of the scene around me, the blue of sky and water, the green of tree and plant, the white of mist and cloud, the purple heather, the gray cliff, the brown or shadowy gorge, the azure of the distant hills, and all these continually varying their hues with the ever-changing light,—I felt that I had drifted clean away from the common-place work-a-day world, and had entered an ideal realm haunted by spirits of beauty and touched with the witchery of an immortal hand. The enthusiasm with which I speak of this mountain-circled lake and these "summer isles of Eden" may appear overcharged to many of my readers, but to such I must say that my poor words limp far behind the actual glories of this Highland loch. This masterpiece of the heavenly Artist is not to be described by the tame vocables of our human speech. Its place of record is the receptive tablets of the memory of the beholder.

> " In spots like these it is we prize
> Our memory, feel that she hath eyes ;
> I feel this place was made for her ;
> To give new pleasure like the past,
> Continued long as life shall last."

I cannot attempt a full description of our voyage over the lake. The first point of call for the steamer is the pretty village of Luss on the western shore. Thence we strike north-east across the lake to Rowardennan, situated at the base of Ben Lomond. The western face of this imposing mountain rises almost immediately from the water's edge. It is said that the view from the summit of the mountain (over 3000 feet high) is wide and rich. One third of Scotland can be seen stretching out below, including Glasgow and Edinburgh ; and beyond Bute and Arran can be descried the distant Atlantic and the coast of Ireland.

As the steamer moves northward along the east shore we pass close to " Rob Roy's Prison," a wall of rock about thirty feet high. This and many other points along the loch have been described by Scott in his fascinating romance of " Rob Roy." From this point we make for Tarbet, situated in a sheltered cove on the west coast. From Tarbet we pursue our zig-zag course towards the eastern shore.

Soon we reach Inversnaid, our port of debarkation, a place of special interest to Canadians on account of its association with a name that they revere,—a place,

too, hallowed by the genius of a great modern poet.
At Inversnaid, in the reign of George II., Major (afterwards General) Wolfe, the victor on the heights of Abraham, was for a time in command of the barracks erected to overawe the restless Macgregors. At Inversnaid, too, Wordsworth saw the "Sweet Highland Girl" whom he has made immortal in one of his most beautiful poems :—

> "Sweet Highland girl, a very shower
> Of beauty is thy earthly dower !
> Twice seven consenting years have shed
> Their utmost bounty on thy head :
> And these gray rocks ; that household lawn ;
> Those trees, a veil just half withdrawn ;
> This fall of water, that doth make
> A murmur near the silent lake ;
> This little bay ; a quiet road
> That holds in shelter thy abode—
> In truth, together do ye seem
> Like something fashioned in a dream ;
> Such forms as from their covert peep
> When earthly cares are laid asleep !
> But, O fair creature, in the light
> Of common day so heavenly bright,
> I bless thee, vision as thou art,
> I bless thee with a human heart."

From Inversnaid we drive—six coach-loads of tourists—eastward through the mountains. About two miles out we pass Rob Roy's cave,—a gloomy hollow amid rugged cliffs. Here Rob Roy and his followers used to make preparations for their southern forays, and here, it is said, Robert Bruce once found a safe asylum.

The road from Inversnaid to Stronachlacher on Loch Katrine skirts the edge of a deep and circuitous ravine.

The scenery on the road is wildly picturesque. Our journey was made exactly at mid-day, but the air was cool and fresh and a heavy mist mantled us about a great part of the way. Reaching the western shore of Loch Katrine we again embark on a little steamer that is to carry us through a region which more than any other has been immortalized by the wonderful genius of Scott. Who has not read "The Lady of the Lake"? Who does not remember the graceful description of Katrine in Canto III. ?—

> "The summer dawn's reflected hue
> To purple changed Loch Katrine blue"—

As the steamer moves eastward you think of Roderick Dhu's course over the little lake as he bears downwards from Glengyle and steers full upon the lonely isle. As you pass the point of Brianchoil you see the spears and pikes and axes of the lawless chief,—the tartans and the bonnets and the plumage of the warriors,—you hear the martial music of the highland pibroch, and catch snatches of the thrilling "Boat Song":

> "Row, vassals, row, for the pride of the Highlands!
> Stretch to your oars, for the ever-green Pine!"

The scenery at the western extremity of the lake is not so beautiful and varied as at the east. All nature among the titanic hills is bare and bleak and desolate. Splintered rocks and massive boulders cover the slopes of the mountains. The shores of the lake are rugged and steep. A fit region this for the exploits of Rob Roy and the Macgregors, for every fastness of these barren shores could tell its terrible tale of suffering and of bloodshed.

As you move eastward the landscape soon takes on fairer and more varied features. Off to the south rises the colossal form of Ben-Venue (2800 feet high). A narrow sheet of water stretches far before you. The coast-lines show many pleasant coves and stretches of pebbled beach. Rustling reeds and waving ferns answer the music of the rippling waves. And yonder is "Ellen's Isle,"—the central point of all, associated with the sweet and cherished memories of "The Lady of the Lake." Yes, this the very retreat to which Ellen Douglas conveyed the Knight of Snowdon, and this is the very refuge of the women and children of the Clan Alpine.

Away to the south, at the base of Ben-Venue, can now be seen the "Goblin's Cave" :—

> "It was a wild and strange retreat,
> As e'er was trod by outlaw's feet.
> The dell, upon the mountain's crest,
> Yawned like a gash on warrior's breast;
> Its trench had stayed full many a rock,
> Hurled by primeval earthquake shock
> From Ben-Venue's gray summit wild."

As I left the little steamer at the narrow eastern inlet of Katrine, and bade good-bye to bold Ben A'an and towering Ben-Venue, to "Ellen's Isle," and the sweet sequestered lake, I snatched some heather, ferns, and flowers from the wayside as souvenirs of these fairy scenes; but the stores of beautiful images that I treasure in my memory will outlast the fading colors and the withering leaves.

And now we take a coach again for a drive through the haunted region of the Trosachs. As the afternoon sun shines in full splendor through the pass, Scott's famous description of this narrow, rugged glen seems wonderfully faithful. At the risk of being tedious I venture to quote a part of the well-known word-picture:

> " The western waves of ebbing day
> Rolled o'er the glen their level way ;
> Each purple peak, each flinty spire,
> Was bathed in floods of living fire.
> But not a setting beam could glow
> Within the dark ravine below,
> Where twined the path in shadow hid,
> Round many a rocky pyramid,
> Shooting abruptly from the dell
> Its thunder-splintered pinnacle ;
> Round many an insulated mass,
> The native bulwarks of the pass,
> Huge as the tower which builders vain
> Presumptuous piled on Shinar's plain.
> The rocky summits, split and rent,
> Formed turret, dome, and battlement,
> Or seemed fantastically set
> With cupola or minaret,
> Wild crests as pagod ever decked,
> Or mosque of Eastern architect.
> Nor were these earth-born castles bare,
> Nor lacked they many a banner fair ;
> For, from their shivered brows displayed,
> Far o'er the unfathomable glade,
> All twinkling with the dew-drop sheen,
> The brier-rose fell in streamers green,
> And creeping shrubs of thousand dyes
> Waved in the west wind's summer sighs."

No other spot in the wide world has been honored with such a description, and as long as the English language lives a never-ending procession of curious travellers will explore this "dark and narrow dell." The intrinsic attractions of the Pass are such as to oppress the beholder with a sense of awe and majesty, and the glamour of poetic glory that the "magician of the north" has cast about it makes its charms more potent still.

The powerful influence of a poet's song has caused a palatial hotel to rise at the eastern limit of the Trosachs. It is a beautiful edifice, stately and turreted, not out of harmony with the sublime scenery within view of it. After a short stay at this Trosachs Hotel our company of tourists proceed by coach along the southern shore of Loch Achray to tne western limit of Loch Vennachar. Here the road turns south, and we follow a very circuitous route through a land of hills, covered with purple heather and dotted with gorse and wild rose bushes. At Aberfoyle we take train for Bucklyvie and thence for Sterling, seeing from the car window the famous castle of Sterling, the ancient seat of Scotland's kings, and passing within sight of the two famous battle-fields of Sterling and Bannockburn. After an hour's delay at Sterling on we rush to Alloa and Dunfermline. Passing over the new bridge over the Frith of Forth—the largest bridge in the world—we steam into Edinburgh at eight o'clock after twelve full and ever-memorable hours.

IV.

EDINBURGH.

> " I view yon Empress of the north
>   Sit on her hilly throne :
> Her palace's imperial bowers,
> Her castle, proof to hostile powers,
> Her stately halls, and holy towers—"

Thus, nearly four centuries ago, on the summit of Blackford Hill, the Lindesay is represented by Scott as having spoken of Edinburgh to Lord Marmion. To-day, though without her frowning ramparts and embattled walls and all her panoply of war Dun-Edin is as fair as ever. Nay, the old streets and ruined palaces enhance her beauty with the pathos of ancient days. Those old-world travellers who have stood upon one of her hills of prospect and have viewed the panorama of her varied charms declare that Edinburgh is the most beautiful city in the world ;—more beautiful even than Naples or Florence or Venice or Rome,—yes, even than brilliant Paris.

The traveller who finds himself in Edinburgh and who is obliged to limit his stay there to a single day, is much perplexed to know how to spend his time to the best advantage, especially if, as was the case with myself, he has neither friend nor acquaintance to accompany him on his rambles to strange scenes and through foreign streets. At nine o'clock on the morning of July 24th I set out alone to explore "Modern Athens," not knowing exactly which way my steps were to turn, but determined to see before nightfall many of the chief places of interest which hitherto I had known only by name.

Passing the Post Office I first proceed to the summit of Calton Hill in the north-east of the city. The view from that lofty eminence is very impressive. Far below are the spires and domes and magnificent structures of the Scottish capital. Wide expanses of rich rural scenery spread far away to the dim hills. In another direction the fine estuary of the Forth broadens out towards the German Ocean. Crowning the rugged brow of Calton Hill are many public monuments, notably Nelson's Monument over one hundred feet high. The National monument, intended to be a copy of the Parthenon at Athens, but for want of funds never completed, is very imposing with its twelve columns.

Descending the hill I pass the High School and the Burns Monument on my way to Arthur's Seat, the highest point in Edinburgh, 822 feet above the sea-level. I take the road so often travelled by Sir Walter Scott past St. Anthony's Chapel,—a fragmentary ruin of a church erected in 1435. Near the ruined chapel is a cool and limpid spring—St. Anthony's Well—whose waters must be tasted by every true tourist. From this point starts the winding path that leads to the distant top of the cliff. After a toilsome ascent I reach the summit of Arthur's seat exactly at noon. On the windy mountain top I sat for a full hour and could have remained there the rest of the day had not the swiftly passing moments warned me that sight-seeing, and not reflections, was my business. A noble passage from the " Chronicles of the Canongate " gives voice to my feelings as I sat musing at mid-day on that lofty crag: " A nobler contrast there can hardly exist than that of the huge city, dark with the smoke of ages, and groaning with the various sounds of active industry or idle revel, and the lofty and craggy hill, silent and solitary as the grave; one exhibiting the full tide of existence pressing and precipitating itself forward with the force of an inundation; the other resembling some time-worn anchorite, whose life passes as silent and unobserved as the slender rill which escapes unheard from the fountain of his patron saint. The city resembles the busy temple, where the modern Comus and Mammon hold their court, and thousands sacrifice ease, independence and virtue itself, at their shrine; the misty and lonely mountain seems as a throne to the majestic but terrible genius of feudal times, where the same divinities dispensed coronets and domains to those who had heads to devise and arms to execute bold enterprises."

With what a feeling of keen regret one leaves this romantic mountain! A last look at the glorious panorama stretched out below—a glance towards the east at the little village containing the inn where tradition says Prince Charles Edward slept before the battle of Prestonpans—another sight of Leith and

Portobello and the blue waters of the Frith, and I descend the steep and barren slopes of Arthur's Seat. Before leaving the base of the mountain I walk along the road that skirts the Salisbury crags,—a favorite walk of Scott and Hume in their daily cogitations.

Between Arthur's seat and Calton Hill are the famous Palace and Abbey of Holyrood. Of the old abbey only some portions of the nave now remain, and an eastern wall built soon after the Reformation. A beautiful ruin is the royal chapel with its Gothic arches, its decorated gateway, its richly sculptured arcade. In the south aisle are deposited the bones of many of the Scottish kings. These well-worn tablets over kings long dead and the crumbling ruins of this ancient abbey carry the mind of the visitor far back into the hoary past, and revive a pathetic interest in struggles and victories and defeats, in rivalries and jealousies, in loves and hates, that once commanded the attention of listening courts and startled realms, but which are now as voiceless and unheeded as the dry dust within this royal vault.

Turning from the Abbey to the Palace adjoining, the visitor is conducted first to the picture gallery containing a series of old Flemish portraits of the Scottish kings. This room was used by Prince Charles Edward in 1745 for his numerous receptions and balls. Readers of "Waverley" will remember the chapter descriptive of "The Ball" and of the brilliant company that met in this room. After the revelry was over, and the musicians had played the signal for parting,—the old air of "Good night, and joy be wi' you a'!", the Prince rose and said : "Good night, and joy be with you !— Good night, fair ladies, who have so highly honored a proscribed and banished Prince.—Good night, my brave friends ; may the happiness we have experienced this evening be an omen of our return to these our paternal halls, speedily and in triumph, and of many and many future meetings of mirth and pleasure in the palace of Holyrood!" Poor, deluded prince ! Culloden Moor was destined next year to blight his hopes forever.

But it is not of Prince Charles that the visitor thinks most when he is within the precincts of the Palace. Mary Queen of Scots must always be the central figure in all the descriptions of Holyrood. Her apartments on the second floor are, it is said, in nearly the same condition as when she inhabited them. Here is the vestibule with the dark stains on the floor, fabled to have been made by the blood of Rizzio, the unfortunate secretary of Mary who was here done to death by the cruel daggers of Darnley and Ruthven. Here is the audience chamber hung with ancient and decaying tapestry, and containing some old chairs adorned with rich embroidery wrought by the hands of Mary and her maids of honor. Here is the spacious and beautiful bed-chamber of the Queen with its gorgeous but faded upholstery. Often did the poor Queen lying on this rich and downy couch feel the full force of King Henry's soliloquy :—

"Why rather, sleep, liest thou in smoky cribs,
Upon uneasy pallets stretching thee,

> Than in the perfumed chambers of the great,
> Under the canopies of costly state,
> And lulled with sounds of sweetest melody?—
> Uneasy lies the head that wears the crown."

On leaving Holyrood I made my way through the Old Town by way of the Canongate and High Street. The Canongate is a street to bewilder the thoughtful traveller who knows its strange history. That history a modern Scotch writer has thus forcibly given : "The Canongate is Scottish history fossilized. What ghosts of kings and queens walk there ! What strifes of steel-clad nobles ! What hurrying of burgesses to man the city walls at the approach of the Southron ! What lamentations over disastrous battle days ! James rode up this street on his way to Flodden. Montrose was dragged up hither on a hurdle, and smote, with disdainful glance, his foes gathered together on the balcony. Jennie Geddes flung her stool at the priest in the church yonder. John Knox came up here to his house after his interview with Mary at Holyrood—grim and stern and unmelted by the tears of a queen. In later days the Pretender rode down the Canongate, his eyes dazzled by the glitter of his father's crown; while bagpipes skirled around, and Jacobite ladies, with white knots in their bosoms, looked down from lofty windows, admiring the beauty of the Prince. Down here of an evening rode Dr. Johnson and Boswell, and turned into the White Horse. David Hume had his dwelling in this street, and trod its pavements. One day a burly ploughman from Ayrshire, with swarthy features and wonderful black eyes, came down here and turned into yonder churchyard to stand with cloudy lids and forehead reverently bared, beside the grave of poor Fergu son. Down this street, too, often limped a little boy, Walter Scott by name, destined in after years to write its "Chronicles." The Canongate once seen is never to be forgotten."

Never to be forgotten ? No,—not for its glorious past, nor for its wretched present ! This is the putrefying sore that mars the wonderful beauty and saps the vigorous vitality of this fair city. Once the abode of the rank, the fashion, the wit, the wealth, the learning, and the beauty of the Scottish capital, the Canongate now teems and swarms with the lowest life of Edinburgh. As I walked up the malodorous street at two o'clock on that bright afternoon of last July, the thoroughfare was thronged with innumerable children, dirty and half naked, while their squalid mothers lolled on doorsteps, or talked in eager groups of the savage pommelling one of their sisterhood had just received at the hands of a drunken termagant. The brutul countenances and the foul tongues of many of these low women dry up in the beholder the fountains of sympathy, but oh, the children !

> "They look up with their pale and sunken faces,
>   And their looks are sad to see,
> For the man's hoary anguish draws an. presses
>   Down the cheeks of infancy."

And this in Edinburgh ! And this in the very centre of Scottish culture and philanthropy ! Are the hands of civilization crippled and palsied that they hang thus limp and idle? Are the tongues of statesmen but as "sounding brass or a tinkling cymbal"? Is sociology to become a living, breathing, throbbing science, keen-eyed and busy-handed, moving amid the haunts of human care and misery, or is she to be merely an idle declaimer, cursing the tyrannies of the past, lamenting the woes of the present, and calmly folding her empty hands as she reveals to weary souls glorious visions of the far-off future?

Just where the Canongate runs into High Street is situated John Knox's house, now over four hundred years old. After viewing the squalor and depravity of the Canongate this peaceful refuge was quieting to the spirit. I was conducted by a guide through the tiny rooms of the old house; I sat in the ancient study-chair of the stern old Reformer; I looked out of the little window from which he used to preach to the Canongate crowds' when he was too feeble to walk to the church of St. Giles near at hand.

Before passing on up High Street I spent a few minutes in Canongate churchyard where Burns came to weep over the grave of the brilliant young Fergusson, his forerunner in Scottish song, who had been cut off at the early age of twenty-three. Burns always called Fergusson "his elder brother in the Muses," and he erected to his memory the memorial-stone still to be seen over his grave and composed the elegy engraved thereon:

"No sculptured marble here, no pompous lay,
 No storied urn, no animated bust.

This simple stone directs pale Scotia's way
To pour her sorrows o'er her poet's dust."

St. Giles' Cathedral is the next place of interest on the way west. This is the oldest church in Edinburgh dating back to the fourteenth century. Here was the scene of the spirited ministry of John Knox. Here Jenny Geddes, in a burst of righteous wrath, hurled her stool at the head of the minister who was enforcing the use of the English liturgy. Here the Solemn League and Covenant was sworn in 1643.

After taking lunch in a plain old-fashioned inn adjoining Greyfriars' Church I passed into the old churchyard of Greyfriars'. Here rests the dust of many old Scottish worthies. A large number of the tombstones have their inscriptions in Latin, a certain indication of their great age. Many of the records have been almost defaced by time. Here are buried Allan Ramsay and Henry Mackenzie, two of Scotland's poets. On the flat monuments in this kirkyard, amid the tears and prayers of the assembled multitude, the Covenant of 1638 was signed. The preacher of the covenanting sermon and the Covenant's enemy, Sir George McKenzie, lie here at rest now side by side. Here, too, near the back of the churchyard are the graves of the covenanting martyrs. I hastily copied a few lines from the old tablet:

"Halt passenger, take heed what you do see,
This tomb doth shew for what some men did die.
Here lies interr'd the dust of those who stood
'Gainst perjury, resisting unto blood."

The inscription goes on to give the names of some of

the principal martyrs, and concludes with the statement that over a hundred of the citizens of Edinburgh were killed by the Government and buried here.

Passing up the Lawnmarket and Castlehill I next visit the Castle of Edinburgh. From whatever point you view the city, its castled rock is the most prominent figure. Scores of cannon frown from the batteries in every direction. The fort is believed to have been a stronghold even in days anterior to the Christian era. All down through the ages the history of Edinburgh has been closely connected with the history of the Castle. The names of Bruce and Baliol and Douglas, of Queen Mary and Cromwell and Prince Charles Edward, of all the Scottish kings through many centuries, are called up by the sight of this hoary citadel.

After leaving the Castle, I search out the Edinburgh residence of Sir Walter Scott from 1800 to 1826, the date of his removal to Abbotsford. The house is a stately building—39 Castle Street—now used as an office by the English and Scottish Investment Co. The only indication that the author of the Waverley Novels ever lived here is a simple marble bust of Sir Walter over the door. As I passed the historic mansion I reflected on the laborious years that the "Magician" spent within these walls,—years (many of them) of dismal debt, but of ever-growing glory.

Scott's Monument on Princess street is the last place I have time to see. It is a fine structure with four large basement arches sustaining a crucial Gothic spire. It is adorned by thirty-two statuettes of characters in Scott's works. The visitor on entering mounts by a circular stair to a room containing many interesting relics—among them some autogragh letters of Scott.

Princes strect, the main thoroughfare of the new city, is the finest street I have ever seen. On one side it is lined by handsome shops, and on the other, for a long distance, by beautiful public gardens. An English traveller has thus written of it : " Here I observed the fairest and goodliest street that ever mine eyes beheld ; for I did never see or hear of a street of the length, the buildings on each side of the way being all of squared stone, five, six, and seven stories high ; and the walls are exceedingly strong, not built for a day, a week, a month, a year, but from antiquity to posterity, for many ages."

Thus I close the account of my solitary excursion through this intensely interesting city,—interesting for its natural and architectural beauty, and for the stirring and touching memories of its sublime and pathetic past.

V.

MELROSE AND ABBOTSFORD.

"If thou would'st view fair Melrose aright,
Go visit it by the pale moonlight;
For the gay beams of lightsome day,
Gild, but to flout, the ruins grey.
When the broken arches are black in night,
And each shafted oriel glimmers white;
When the cold light's uncertain shower
Streams on the ruin'd central tower;
When buttress and buttress, alternately,
Seemed framed of ebon and ivory;
When silver edges the imagery,
And the scrolls that teach thee to live and die;
When distant Tweed is heard to rave,
And the owlet to hoot o'er the dead man's grave;
Then go—but go alone the while—
Then view St. David's ruin'd pile;
And, home returning, soothly swear,
Was never scene so sad and fair."

Thus in the "Lay of the Last Minstrel" Scott instructs the visitor to Melrose. However desirous of viewing the abbey aright I was not able to arrange for a moonlight visit; but necessity drove me to "go alone the while." Although I saw the grey ruins under "the gay beams of lightsome day," I am prepared to acknowledge, if not soothly to swear, that the scene is indeed "sad and fair."

At nine o'clock in the morning, July 25th, I left Edinburgh, taking train by the Waverley line of the

North British Railway. A journey of 37 miles in a south-easterly direction past Portobello and Galashiels brought me to the little town of Melrose, and to a region which was the scene of much fierce fighting in the old Border days, and which has been gilded with a halo of romantic glory by the author of "The Monastery," and "The Lay."

Melrose Abbey, adjacent to the little town of Melrose, was founded in 1136 by King David the First. When Edward II. retreated from Scotland in 1322 the English despoiled the abbey. It was restored by King Robert Bruce in 1326. Although in 1384 the chancel of the church was burned by Richard II. of England, and in 1544 the whole abbey was fired by an emissary of Henry VIII., still the present roofless ruins are mainly those of the old monastery built nearly six centuries ago. The abbey is now in the possession of the noble house of Buccleuch and great care is being taken to preserve the venerable ruins from further decay.

Melrose Abbey is cruciform in shape like so many of the Gothic abbeys and cathedrals of Europe. The visitor is admitted by the custodian at the abbey gate situated at the west end of the south aisle. The first six of the chapels in the south aisle have been used ever since the Reformation as burial-places by noted families in the vicinity. The visitor as he enters sees, in the very first chapel on the right, high up on the wall, the following impressive inscription which must serve as a specimen of the many to be found in every part of the ruined church :

> THE DUST OF MANY GENERATIONS OF THE
> BOSTONS OF GATTONSIDE IS DEPOSITED IN
> THIS PLACE. WE GIVE OUR BODIES TO
> THIS HOLY ABBEY TO KEEP.

Melrose Abbey contains some very fine specimens of Gothic sculpture. The south transept in particular is distinguished for the beauty of its foliage tracery and of its quaintly carved figures. The wasting elements have dealt roughly with the marble leaves and flowers, but enough remains to attest the exquisite taste and skill of the sculptors whose cunning hands, in centuries long past, fashioned these magnificent designs.

At the east end of the south transept, and separated from it by three pillars, is St. Bridget's Chapel, which here receives mention on account of a curious relic that it contains. When in 1649 the fiat of Cromwell demolished the images in so many churches, Melrose Abbey did not escape. In St. Bridget's Chapel, however, may still be seen a statue of that saint standing on a pedestal in a niche near one of the windows. The wanton myrmidons of the Protector failed to notice and to destroy this insignificant image of one of the minor saints. The little statue, grimy and mutilated, stands staring stonily from its sheltered recess and with dumb eloquence telling of the glorious days when every niche in these crumbling walls had its image of saint or martyr.

Between St. Bridget's Chapel and the chancel at the east is a short aisle which was probably used as a separate chapel. This corner of the abbey is the focus of attraction for all visitors to Melrose. Here, according to the "Lay of the Last Minstrel," is the grave of the famous wizard, Michael Scott, whose magic words cleft into three the Eildon Hills, which, on the south of the abbey, rise majestically from a common base to three tall summits. Readers of the "Lay" will remember the impressive scene in the second canto where Deloraine stands over the open grave of Michael Scott and a supernatural light streams up from the vault to the chancel roof :

> " No earthly flame blazed e'er so bright ;
> It shone like heaven's own blessed light."

William of Deloraine had been sent hither by the Ladye of Branksome to secure the wizard's "Mighty Book" of spells and enchantments ; but, as he saw the dead magician with a silver cross in his right hand, "his Book of Might" in his left, and a ghostly lamp placed by his knees, the steady-hearted and stout-handed warrior stood bewildered and unnerved.

Standing near the fabled grave of Michael Scott you have in full view the famous eastern window of Melrose Abbey, which has received a splendid tribute in the "Lay of the Last Minstrel" :

> " The moon on the east oriel shone.
> Through slender shafts of shapely stone,
>   By foliage tracery combined ;
> Thou would'st have thought some fairy's hand
> 'Twixt poplars straight the osier wand,
>   In many a freakish knot, had twined ;
> Then framed a spell when the work was done,
> And changed the willow wreaths to stone."

Under the floor of the chancel, just below the beautiful window, repose the ashes of many illustrious personages. Alexander II. was buried here. Here were interred the bodies of William Douglas, ".the dark Knight of Liddesdale," and of James Douglas, slain by Hotspur at the battle of Otterburn in 1388. Here, too, tradition say is deposited the heart of King Robert Bruce, brought back from Spain after Douglas had attempted unsuccessfully to carry it to the Holy Land.

After passing through the north transept and viewing the sacristy you proceed to the north aisle, conspicuous for the beauty of its pointed roof and massive pillars. In this aisle, just beyond the cloister door, there is an ancient inscription on the wall, remarkable for its touching simplicity and for the admiration bestowed on it by Washington Irving. It reads as follows :

> HEIR LYIS THE RACE
> OF YE HOVS OF ZAIR.

Right opposite this inscription are seen the tombs of the ancient family of Karr, or Kerr.

At this point you may pass into the cloisters through the exquisitely carved door mentioned in the "Lay":

> "By a steel-clenched postern door,
> They entered now the chancel tall."

As the visitor passes from the cloisters towards the grand south entrance on his way out he will get the most imposing view of the interior of the ruined monastery. Now, too, will come on him in full flood a current of associations and influences that will make him linger long on the bright green turf that forms the summer floor of the western portion of the nave. What scenes of holy rapture and of unholy ravage have been enacted within these sacred walls! What tears of moaning penitents and blood of slaughtered priests have consecrated yon cold grey stones! What holy hymns of virgins and wanton shouts of pitiless soldiers have been re-echoed through these ancient aisles! What a multitude of venerable abbots and cowled monks, of mailed warriors and gallant knights and high-born dames, worshipped here in the olden days before the pillared arches and the fretted roof had fallen in ruins! And beneath these hard, rough slabs and this well-packed clay and even this daisied turf lie the mortal remains of how many royal and historic figures!

As I left Melrose Abbey and bade good-bye to the intelligent and courteous custodian I could not but reflect that nearly all of the great procession of tourists who come here by the hundred every day have been attracted to the spot not by the intrinsic beauties of the ruined church however great they are, but by the genius of the poet and novelist who used frequently to visit the old abbey, to gaze upon yon eastern window, or to take his favorite seat on yonder stone by the grave of the old wizard who bore the same surname,— Scott.

ABBOTSFORD.

In 1811 Walter Scott purchased a tract of land on the bank of the Tweed about three miles west of Melrose. He was led to the purchase by several considerations. The Tweed at this point is a beautiful river, flowing broad and bright over a pebbly bed. Another feature of interest at the time was an old Roman road leading from the Eildon Hills to the ford over the river adjoining the estate. Besides, the picturesque ruins of Melrose Abbey are visible from many points in the immediate neighborhood. At one time the land had belonged to the Abbey of Melrose, as might be inferred from the name of *Abbotsford*. The small house which was on the estate at the time of purchase Scott gradually enlarged and improved, but some years later the old structure was torn down and the present palatial mansion was erected on its site.

After leaving Melrose Abbey I started at noon to walk to Abbotsford by a picturesque road that runs not far from the high banks of the Tweed. This was my first country walk in Britain, and many things contributed to make it delightful. The highway, like nearly all British roads, runs between two lines of hawthorn hedges. Peeping out from the hedgerows were pretty wild roses and blue-bells. The foot-path by the roadside was hard and clean. The air was balmy and exhilarating. The prospect was everywhere beautiful. Off to the left, rising 1200 feet high, were the three peaks of the Eildon Hills. To the right flowed the romantic Tweed. The only distraction on the road was the frequent passage of coachloads of tourists bound for Abbotsford or returning therefrom. After I had walked two miles I began to peer ahead for the world-famed mansion of Sir Walter, but not a glimpse of it was to be seen until the gateway was reached. I had expected to find Abbotsford on some commanding slope,—a place to be seen for miles around. I found it snugly situated on meadowland very close to the river.

Abbotsford is now the property of Lady Hope-Scott, the great-grand-daughter of the founder of the house. Lady Scott occupies part of the house during the summer months, but all the rooms of public interest are open to visitors every lawful day. Abbotsford has been styled "a romance in stone and lime," as it exhibits combinations of architecture after Sir Walter's original and antiquarian tastes. It is said to embody in its structure copies of portions of Melrose Abbey, Roslin Chapel, Holyrood Palace, Linlithgow Palace, and other admired buildings. It is now practically a grand public museum of antiquities, arts, and literature, and it contains many relics of Sir Walter's dress, habits, and pursuits.

The cicerone who conducts the visitor through Sir Walter's rooms has been happily chosen. She has sad eyes and a very plaintive voice, both conducive to a suitable spirit of repose and reverence in those whom she guides and instructs. A bold, harsh tone and flippant manner would be a desecration in these hallowed rooms.

Visitors are rapidly conducted in companies of about twenty through the various rooms, the guide pointing out all objects of special interest as you proceed. In turn we pass through the gorgeous library with its thirty-thousand volumes; the neat drawing-room with its rich upholstery and beautiful pictures; the armory with its marvellous collection of guns, swords, daggers, and countless relics of antiquarian interest; the entrance hall, sumptuously furnished with a museum-like collection of curiosities and antiquities; and lastly the study, containing the desk and chair used by Sir Walter during the years of the production of many of the Waverley Novels.

How pathetic were Scott's last days in this splendid mansion! By the failure of his publishers saddled with a debt of a hundred and seventeen thousand pounds he set himself proudly and bravely to pay it off. He worked day by day at his Hercules' task cheerfully and unweariedly. "While his life strings were cracking, he grappled with it, and wrestled with it, years long, in death grips, strength to strength;—and it proved the stronger; and his life and heart did crack and break; the cordage of a most strong heart." Let me conclude this chapter with another sentence from Carlyle:—"When he departed he took a Man's life along with him. No sounder piece of British manhood was put together in that eighteenth century of time. Ah, his fine Scotch face, we shall never forget it; we shall never see it again. Adieu, Sir Walter, pride of all Scotchmen, take our proud and sad farewell."

VI.

LONDON—ST. PAUL'S CATHEDRAL AND WESTMINSTER ABBEY.

When in the early morning of July 26th, after an all-night journey from Scotland, I drew near to the metropolis of the world, I had none of the eagerness of the boy in "Locksley Hall" who travelling by night along the dusky highway and drawing nearer and nearer to the world's capital at last "sees in heaven the light of London flaring like a dreary dawn," and who joyfully leaps forward in spirit to mingle among the throngs of men. Among the four millions of people I knew not one, nor had I the vaguest conception of the topography of the place. When the guard at the railway station shouted out the most familiar name in the vocabulary of cities, all the friendliness and melody of the word vanished and it sounded like a knell. Life was fully astir in the great city and clamorous labor was stretching out his hundred hands. Weary and depressed I longed to be away in some dense forest or on some trackless mountain,

> "But midst the crowd, the hum, the shock of men,
> To hear, to see, to feel, and to possess,
> With none who bless us, none whom we can bless,—
> This is to be alone; this, this is solitude."

Taking a hansom I soon found a place of shelter—but by no means a quiet refuge—at the Norfolk Hotel, near the busy and noisy Strand, in the very heart of the throbbing, roaring, feverish life of London.

Sleep and rest soon restored my normal buoyancy of spirits, and short excursions in different directions soon familiarized me with my novel environment. The Strand and Fleet Street, Blackfriars' Bridge and The Thames, Charing Cross, and Pall Mall, soon threw aside their frown and assumed a friendly aspect. Everything of public interest which I have to record in connection with my first four days in London will be reserved for a subsequent chapter on London life. The present chapter is to be devoted to a brief description of two of London's most interesting churches,— interesting not mainly as churches, but as repositories of the bones of England's mighty dead.

ST. PAUL'S CATHEDRAL.

The history of St. Paul's dates back to the seventh century and the times of Ethelbert, King of Kent. The church was destroyed by fire in the tenth century and again in the eleventh century. The third edifice, a magnificent structure, was destroyed by the great fire of 1666. The present cathedral is a monument to the architectural genius of Sir Christopher Wren. He spent 35 years of his life in overseeing the erection of the building, the first stone being laid in 1675 and the last in 1710.

St. Paul's Cathedral is 500 feet long from east to west and 250 feet broad at the transept. The height of the building is 352 feet from the floor to the top of the cross. The Cathedral covers more than two acres of ground. Its aggregate cost was nearly four million dollars.

In the various aisles and transepts of St. Paul's are to be seen the monuments of many illustrious men. The visitor, as he scans the monumental inscriptions, cannot fail to be impressed with a strange and startling contrast. Here we read of deans and bishops who have been consecrated to declare the glad evangel of peace on earth and good will toward men : there, in close proximity, are marble tablets that announce the glorious triumphs of generals and of admirals whose hands have been stained with the blood of hundreds of their slaughtered countrymen and thousands of their hated foes. "My house shall be called the house of prayer, but ye have made it "—a temple for the deification of the cannon ball and the reeking sword. Some of these national heroes, it is true, have sacrificed their lives to save Britain from the heel of the oppressor, but alas ! too many have gone down to death in unholy crusades and wanton wars.

A very interesting part of the great cathedral is the Crypt. In the south aisle is the Painters' Corner where lie the remains of many of those great artists whose easels have adorned the drawing-rooms and picture galleries of an appreciative kingdom. Sir Joshua

Reynolds and West and Lawrence and Turner and Landseer have all been honored with burial here.

In the very centre of the Crypt is the sarcophagus of black marble containing the remains of Lord Nelson. Near at hand is another huge sarcophagus of porphyry bearing the inscription :

ARTHUR, DUKE OF WELLINGTON,

Born May 1st, 1769, died September 14th, 1852.

However one may deplore the hideous horrors of war and may yearn for an era of universal peace and human brotherhood, it is impossible to view these two mausoleums of the heroes of Trafalgar and Waterloo without a throb of national pride. What a noble ode is that of Tennyson's on the Death of Wellington,—an ode that shines as well with the lustre of Nelson's fame :

> "Thine island loves thee well, thou famous man,
> The greatest sailor since our world began.
> Now, to the roll of muffled drums,
> To thee the greatest soldier comes ;
> For this is he
> Was great by land as thou by sea."
> * * * *
> "Where shall we lay the man whom we deplore ?
> Here, in streaming London's central roar.
> Let the sound of those he wrought for,
> \nd the feet of those he fought for,
> Echo round his bones for evermore."—
>
> "Under the cross of gold
> That shines over city and river,
> There he shall rest forever
> Among the wise and the bold."

After leaving the Crypt the visitor ascends to the Whispering Gallery by a stair of 260 steps. This gallery, circular in form, is 420 feet in circumference, yet it is so constructed that the least whisper is heard from one side to the other as if it were a loud voice close to your ear.

The next place of interest is the Stone Gallery surrounding the dome. From this great height one has a fine view of the vast metropolis far below. The guide conducts you around the dome, over 200 feet above the street level, and points out the chief objects of interest in the impressive panorama that stretches beyond the vision on every side. What a huge, mighty, tremendous city this wonderful London is ?

The visitor must not come away from St. Paul's without seeing the Library with its 12,000 volumes, many of them very old. Nor should he forget the Great Bell which is said to weigh 12,000 lbs. The gorgeous Reredos in the cathedral should also be seen : the sculptured work is of white Parian marble, the figures representing incidents in the life of Christ.

During my ten days' stay in London I passed St. Paul's Cathedral many times, but never without some emotion, and never without gazing at that marvellous dome which gives to liliputian mortals a greater idea of height than the azure dome of the familiar sky.

WESTMINSTER ABBEY.

To the student of history and literature no spot in all London is so attractive as Westminster Abbey. I had read graphic descriptions of the old abbey written by the hands of such masters as Goldsmith and Addison and Washington Irving. I was thus fittingly prepared for my visit to the ancient building. With reverence and awe I entered its portals. The lofty roof and the noble range of pillars and all the beauties of architectural design are almost unnoticed by one who reflects that he is here surrounded "by the congregated bones of the great men of past times, who have filled history with their deeds, and the earth with their renown."

Roaming about through the aisles and chapels I saw on pavements and on walls countless memorials of departed greatness. Familiar names of every rank and profession and opinion are crowded and packed together. Here are monuments to the memory of Fox and the two Pitts, of Newton and Herschel, of Wilberforce and Livingstone, of Darwin and Kingsley and Wordsworth, of Keble and Watts and the Wesleys, and of hosts of others who have performed great deeds or have recorded such deeds in imperishable words.

I must not allow myself to attempt a description of the famous chapel of Henry VII. I must call to my assistance the glowing periods of Washington Irving: "Great gates of brass, richly and delicately wrought, turn heavily upon their hinges, as if proudly reluctant to admit the feet of common mortals into this most gorgeous of sepulchres. On entering, the eye is astonished by the pomp of architecture, and the elaborate beauty of sculptured detail. The very walls are wrought into universal ornament, incrusted with tracery, and scooped into niches, crowded with the statues of saints and martyrs. Stone seems, by the cunning labor of the chisel, to have been robbed of its weight and density, suspended aloft as if by magic, and the fretted roof achieved with the wonderful minuteness and airy security of a cobweb. Along the sides of the chapel are the lofty stalls of the Knights of the Bath, richly carved of oak, though with the grotesque decorations of Gothic architecture. On the pinnacles of the stalls are affixed the helmets and crests of the knights, with their scarfs and swords; and above them are suspended their banners, emblazoned with armorial bearings, and contrasting the splendor of gold and purple and crimson with the cold gray fretwork of the roof. In the midst of this grand mausoleum stands the sepulchre of its founder,—his effigy, with that of his queen, extended on a sumptuous tomb, and the whole surrounded by a superbly wrought brazen railing."

"Two small aisles on each side of this chapel present a touching instance of the equality of the grave, which brings down the oppressor, and mingles the dust of the bitterest enemies together. In one is the sepulchre of the haughty Elizabeth; in the other is that of her victim, the lovely and unfortunate Mary. A peculiar melancholy reigns over the aisle where Mary lies buried. The light struggles dimly through windows darkened by dust. The greater part of the place is in deep shadow, and the walls are stained and tinted by time and weather. A marble figure of Mary is stretched upon the tomb, round which is an iron railing, much corroded, bearing her national emblem—the thistle."

In one of the aisles of the chapel of Henry VII. is a curious little tomb which must not escape mention. It is a marble child in a stone cradle, erected to the memory of Sophia, the infant princess of James I., who died when three days old :

> " A little rudely sculptured bed,
>   With shadowing folds of marble lace,
> And quilt of marble primly spread
>   And folded round a baby's face.
>
> But dust upon the cradle lies,
>   And those who prized the baby so,
> And laid her down to rest with sighs,
>   Were turned to dust long years ago.
>
> Above the peaceful pillowed head
>   Three centuries brood, and strangers peep
> And wonder at the carven bed,—.
>   But not unwept the baby's sleep."

The chapel of Edward the Confessor carries the mind back to very ancient days. A mere catalogue of the kings and queens who lie buried here would bewilder or fatigue my patient readers. One object of interest in this part of the abbey must, however, not be overlooked. Here is to be seen the Coronation Chair, rudely carved of oak and enclosing the stone that was brought with the regalia from Scotland by Edward I. and offered to St. Edward's shrine in the year 1297. In this chair all the reigning sovereigns of England have been crowned since that remote period.

In the Chapel of St. John is an impressive tomb which has excited the comments of visitors to the abbey for a hundred and fifty years. The tomb was made by that eminent statuary, Roubiliac, in memory of Lady Elizabeth Nightingale who died at the early age of twenty-seven. "The bottom of the monument [I quote from the Sketch Book] is represented as throwing open its marble doors, and a sheeted skeleton is starting forth. The shroud is falling from his fleshless form as he launches his dart at his victim. She is sinking into her affrighted husband's arms, who strives with vain and frantic effort to avert the blow. The whole is executed with terrible truth and spirit; we almost fancy we hear the gibbering yell of triumph bursting from the distended jaws of the spectre. But why should we thus seek to clothe death with unnecessary terrors, and to spread horrors round the tomb of those we love? The grave should be surrounded by everything that might inspire tenderness and veneration for the dead, or that might win the living to virtue. It is the place, not of disgust and dismay, but of sorrow and meditation."

The corner of the abbey for which I shall retain the tenderest memories I now notice last of all. Some recent verses of Aldrich on The Poets' Corner are so sweetly appreciative that I cannot forbear to quote them :

"Tread softly here; the sacredest of tombs
Are those that hold your poets. Kings and queens
Are facile accidents of Time and Chance;
Chance sets them on the heights, they climb not there!
But he who from the darkling mass of men
Is on the wing of heavenly thought upbore
To finer ether, and becomes a voice
For all the voiceless, God anointed him!
His name shall be a star, his grave a shrine.

Tread softly here, in silent reverence tread,
Beneath those marble cenotaphs and urns
Lies richer dust than ever nature hid
Packed in the mountain's adamantine heart,
Or slyly wrapt in unsuspecting sand.
The dross men toil for often stains the soul.
How vain and all ignoble seems the greed
To him who stands in this dim cloistered air
With these most sacred ashes at his feet!

This dust was Chaucer, Spenser, Dryden this;
The spark that once illumed it lingers still.
O, ever-hallowed spot of English earth!
If the unleashed and happy spirit of man
Have option to revisit our dull globe,
What august shades at midnight here convene
In the miraculous sessions of the moon,
When the great pulse of London faintly throbs,
And one by one the stars in heaven pale!"

I passed two pensive hours in Poets' Corner. I lingered long beside the tombs of my favorite poets. I felt that here even in a strange land I was among friends and companions, whose frail bodies, it is true, had long been dust, but whose spirits having flown over sea and continent and having graciously communed with mine in many a silent hour of exquisite delight now seemed to fill this holy air with the mysterious magnetism of their unseen but friendly presence.

The poets have welcomed to their corner of the abbey many whose genius has not been mainly that of song. The claims of the actor, the musician, the historian, and the novelist, to a kinship with the illustrious poets have been recognized and honored in the persons of Garrick, and Handel, and Macaulay, and Dickens, whose perishing remains lie at rest forever beneath these marble slabs.

The Poets' Corner—may it last with this glorious abbey from age to age, to remind us of those who have made us heirs of so many noble truths and pure de lights,—to soften natures growing hard with the dull routine of care,—to inspire many generations of youthful singers to the highest exertion of their native powers.

But as I sat in Westminster Abbey in the waning hours of the final day of last July, facing the marble figure of the gentle Shakespeare, I was not allowed to forget that the gigantic pile that towered above me would one day share the fate of the mighty temples of ancient days, and would perhaps " with the process of the suns" perish from record and from recollection. On the scroll that adorns the monument of the immortal dramatist are chiselled these prophetic words from "The Tempest":

> " The cloud-capp'd towers, the gorgeous palaces,
> The solemn temples, the great globe itself,
> Yea, all which it inherit, shall dissolve,
> And, like the baseless fabric of a vision,
> Leave not a rack behind."

VII.

LONDON.

A Canadian visitor in London who has only about a week to spend in the metropolis has a perplexing problem continually on hand. Here is a city whose history dates back to the time of Cæsar and every street of which is rich with the traditions and stories of an ancient past. To follow the guiding of the historian or archæologist and traverse the old streets and alleys of the city in search of spots that have gained undying renown on account of their association with illustrious personages or famous events, would require months instead of days. Moreover, modern London, if we disregard entirely its interesting past, is a city so vast and of such varied attractions that a year is all too short for surveying it with any degree of thoroughness. Whatever objects of interest, however, one can afford to leave unvisited, there are some places whose claims are paramount. The museums and picture-galleries and gardens of London, which private enterprise or public munificence have endowed, are to curious travellers from over the sea not only places of pleasing entertainment, but also great schools that impart much useful knowledge to be gained nowhere else under the sun. Whatever disadvantages life in this swarming hive of human industry may have, there are inestimable advantages from which all but Londoners are quite cut off. A series of visits to such famous institutions as I mention in this chapter must give to many of the intelligent inhabitants of London a liberal education.

THE ZOOLOGICAL GARDENS.

Two miles north-west from the Strand in a corner of Regent's Park is situated the favorite resort of London children,—The Zoological Gardens, called in familiar parlance "The Zoo." Here is to be seen the largest collection of animals in the world. All creatures that frequent the jungles of trackless forests, that fly in the illimitable air, that wade or swim in lakes and rivers, that haunt the deep places of the sea, have been brought by man from their familiar habitats and have been here provided, as far as possible, with all their native surroundings. Many of the animals, indeed, have been born in the Gardens, and so know only by instinctive restlessness that they are not at home here in the centre of populous London.

It would be useless to give my readers a catalogue of the beasts, birds and fishes that throng these famous Gardens. Even to name the various houses, or sections, of the Gardens would serve no useful purpose. I may say, however, that there is one house through which I hurried with swift steps,—the house containing hundreds of those creeping monsters that were doomed by the original curse to eat dust forever and to be forever bruised and hated by man. There is another section of the Gardens which attracted me as much as the snakes repelled me ;—the Aviary with its hundreds of birds of beautiful plumage and melodious song. Here I was much pleased to see two of my Canadian friends,—the cunning robin and the pretty bluebird. These appear to be the only two songsters that represent the abundant avifauna of Canada in this vast ornithological collection.

MADAME TUSSAUD'S.

Who was Madame Tussaud ? In her day she was a very remarkable woman. While yet a girl, at her uncle's table in Paris she used to meet many men afterwards famous in French life and history,—Voltaire, Rousseau, Robespierre and Mirabeau. After the Reign of Terror she married, but her union was an unfortunate one. Friendless and deserted she left France and landed in London alone without a penny. The happy thought struck her that she might make use of the art of modelling in wax which she had learned in her girlhood. She soon formed a museum of wax casts of contemporary celebrities. The enterprise was successful from the start and her exhibition of waxworks and French relics became one of the most popular attractions of the English capital. For nearly a hundred years this place of entertainment and instruction has been growing in dimensions and attractiveness. Madame Tussaud was succeeded in the management by her sons, and the exhibition now belongs to her great-grandchildren.

One's expectations of a waxwork show are naturally not very lofty. Designing in wax is a form of art not to be compared to the art of the sculptor. A visit, however, to Madame Tussaud's will quickly change depreciation to admiration. I cannot go quite the length of a recent traveller to Britain who asserts that this exhibition is the most impressive thing in London. Still I am ready to admit that I was surprised and astonished at the wonderful collection of lifelike statues that fill every corner of the large building. Nearly every famous personage, living and dead, is here represented in wax. The figures are so true to life that it is often difficult to distinguish the statues from the gazing spectators. The effect is somewhat startling when you are here confronted by the image of one whom you may have seen in the flesh but a few days before.

There is one part of this exhibition which I advise those of fine sensibility to avoid,—the "Chamber of Horrors." Here in the dim light of the basement you pass the hideous figures of many bloody criminals whose terrible deeds have gained for them a brief notoriety. In the dungeon-like darkness of these dusty chambers your flesh creeps and your pulse throbs and you carry away with you as you hastily depart many mental pictures which may disturb your waking hours and haunt your midnight dreams for many a day to come.

To me one of the most interesting features of Madame Tussaud's is the section called the " Napoleon

Rooms." Here are collected a great number of invaluable French relics, most of them associated with the name of the great Emperor. Here is the huge military carriage used by Napoleon in his Russian campaign, and captured by the British on the evening of Waterloo. Here is the camp bedstead of Napoleon used for six years at St. Helena,—with the mattresses and the pillow on which he died. Here is the sword carried by the great soldier in his Egyptian campaign. The numerous articles of historic bric-a-brac contained in the "Napoleon Rooms" are alone sufficient to draw readers of history to the Tussaud Museum.

THE CRYSTAL PALACE.

A journey of about eight miles from Ludgate Hill brings you to that famous museum and pleasure resort, —The Crystal Palace, designed and laid out about forty years ago by Sir Joseph Paxton. The various courts, houses, vestibules and galleries of this wonderful exhibition are filled with interesting objects connected with every science and every art. My visit to the Palace on the evening of July 31st gave me time for only a cursory view of the permanent parts of the exhibition. That evening was a special occasion called "Children's Night." Over ten thousand people, half of them boys and girls, had come out from the crowded city to see the fireworks and the ballet. The display of pyrotechnics that fascinated the great crowd for about an hour was gorgeous indeed. Illuminated balloons, ascending clouds of gold, aerial festoons, whistling rockets, beautiful designs in fiery colors shifting and gleaming in kaleidoscopic splendor, made the extensive gardens a fairyland of beauty. I shall never forget the scene when at the close the whole place was lighted up for an instant by the discharge of a great magnesium shell and ten thousand bright and eager faces looked up into the illuminated sky.

Immediately after the fireworks came the ballet which held the attention of the great throng for another hour. I quote from a London paper of Aug. 2nd an appreciative description of the magnificent spectacle : " A prettier sight cannot be seen than an open-air ballet at the Crystal Palace, and, now that summer has come, and the pastoral players can venture forth without fear of rheumatic fever, 'The Witches' Haunt' should draw thousands to Sydenham. Nothing quite so enchanting as this ballet have the managers succeeded in producing on their al-fresco stage. 'Rip Van Winkle' and 'A Midsummer Night's Dream' have had some share in inspiring this exquisite fancy, but no theatre could rival the beauties of its natural setting. Miniature cascades, mountains and dells, the very home of weird and ghostly elves, lie in the hollow, a sylvan scene of indescribable loveliness; and haunting effects, grotesque and beautiful and fantastic, are passed before us with bewildering rapidity, by the aid of the electrician and the dainty art of the costumier. The story of the ballet is simplicity itself, merely the sleep of an adventurous young forester and his introduction to the inhabitants of the wood, but it serves as a peg upon which to hang original dances, the most ingenious groupings, and hundreds of ravishing tints. Madame Lanner's children are now quite an institution, and their grace and charm and obvious love for their work on Wednesday night called forth the customary confessions of admiration and delight."

THE NATIONAL GALLERY.

A distinguished authority, Mr. Ruskin, says that the National Gallery is, for the purposes of the general student, the most important collection of paintings in Europe. The Gallery was instituted in 1824 and has been steadily growing ever since. Most of the pictures have been purchased out of the public funds, some of them at very great expense, a single picture of Raphael's —the "Ansidei Madonna"—having cost $350,000. It is said that the collection now contains 1,050 pictures.

I had only three hours to spend in the National Gallery and I occupied nearly the whole time in the apartments devoted to the British School. Turner's pictures alone, filling a large room, cannot be examined in less than an hour.

No two visitors to the National Gallery would select the same pictures for special mention. The following are those that held my attention longest :—

"The Graces decorating a Statue of Hymen" by Joshua Reynolds—the Graces being represented by three beautiful daughters of an English nobleman of the day.—

"The Earl of Chatham's Last Speech" by Copley, representing a scene that took place in the House of Lords in 1778, when Chatham after a great speech sank down in an apoplectic fit.—

"Youth on the Prow and Pleasure at the Helm" by Etty, depicting in glowing colors a word-picture in Gray's Bard.—

"Doctor Johnson in Lord Chesterfield's Ante-Room" by Ward.—

"Childe Harold's Pilgrimage" by Turner, representing a composite Italian scene,—a very paradise of loveliness.—

"The Maid and the Magpie" by Landseer, of delicate design and flaming color.—

"The Preaching of John Knox" by Wilkie—a scene in the parish church at St. Andrew's before the angry prelates and nobles of Scotland.—

"An Equestrian Portrait of Charles I." by Van Dyck, one of the most striking of the Flemish pictures.

"Heads of Angels" by Reynolds, the printed copies of which give no suggestion of the richness of the original.—

"The Rape of the Sabines" by Rubens, one of the boldest of the classical pictures, having a touch of grossness about it.—

"The Judgment of Paris" also by Rubens, displaying much of his sensuous realism.—

"Lord Byron's Dream" by Eastlake, illustrating Byron's wonderful poem, "The Dream."—

"A Distinguished Member of the Humane Society" by Landseer,—a large Newfoundland dog with human pathos in his eyes.

But my list is long enough. A descriptive catalogue of great pictures by great artists must be very uninviting in the absence of the glow of colors, the mysteries of light and shade, and the magical symmetry of beautiful forms.

THE BRITISH MUSEUM.

Oliver Wendell Holmes gives some sage advice in regard to inspecting the British Museum. If you wish not to see it, he says, drop into the building when you have a spare hour at your disposal, and wander among its books and its various collections: you will then know as much about it as the fly that buzzes in at one window and out at another. If you wish to see the British Musuem, he says, take lodgings next door to it and pass all your days at the museum during the whole period of your natural life : at threescore and ten you will have some faint conception of the contents, significance, and value of this great British institution. The same writer says "There is one lesson to be got from a short visit to the British Museum,—namely, the fathomable abyss of our own ignorance : one is crushed by the vastness of the treasures in the library and the collection of this universe of knowledge."

I am not going to take my readers through the Egyptian, Assyrian, or Etruscan rooms of this wonderful place, nor must I ask them to follow me through the Greek and Roman Rooms, where I wandered for two hours. The King's Library, with its 65,000 volumes donated by George IV., must prove interesting to all visitors. The Manuscript Saloon is to me the most interesting quarter of the Museum. It contains autograph letters of all the English sovereigns from Richard II. to Victoria and of nearly all the great literary men of England and France. It brings one very near to these magnates of royalty and literature to see the very words that their pens have formed and the very paper over which their warm hands of flesh have moved. A few characteristic touches from some of these letters, which I copied down in my pocket note-book, I here transcribe. I have seen none of these extracts in printed books, and so they will be new to most of my readers.

A letter from Cromwell to his wife begins : "My Deerest, I praise the Lord I am encreased in strength in my outward Man."

Shelley to Miss Curran : "My dear Miss Curran— I ought to have written to you some time ago, but my ill spirits and ill health has forever furnished me with an excuse for delaying till to-morrow. I fear that you still continue too capable of justly estimating my apology."

Dickens to a friend the day before his own death, on being invited to a feast, writes : "These violent delights often have violent ends."

Browning to a friend (Nov. 1868) : "I can have little doubt but that my writing has been, in the main, too hard for many, but I never designedly tried to puzzle people. I never pretended to offer a substitute for a cigar or a game of dominoes to an idle man."

Wordsworth to ———— : " I deferred answering your very obliging letter till my visit to this place should give me an opportunity of a Frank " (! !).

Lamb to a Friend : " Since I saw you I have been in France and have eaten frogs—the nicest little rabbity things I ever tasted."

Pope : " This letter, Dear Sir, will be extremely laconic."

Voltaire, (written at Geneva in good English by himself)—" Had I not fixed the seat of my retreat in the free corner of Geneva, I would certainly live in the free Kingdom of England."

Nelson to Lady Hamilton (his last letter on the eve of Trafalgar) : at the end of the letter are these words in Lady Hamilton's handwriting—" Oh, miserable, wretched Emma—Oh, glorious and happy Nelson."

SOUTH KENSINGTON MUSEUM.

The wealth of interest that this museum contains is quite as great for the general visitor as that of the British Museum. Such a collection of works of art and wonders of all kinds can be found nowhere out of London. I can here only indicate very briefly a few of the objects that impressed me most.

The Raphael Gallery contains the celebrated Raphael cartoons, drawn in chalk on strong paper. These cartoons, twelve feet in height, were originally drawn as copies for tapestries to be worked in wool, silk and gold, and to adorn the Sistine Chapel at Rome.

The Sheepshanks collection of pictures contains many important works by Turner, Landseer, Wilkie, Leslie, Constable, Mulready, and other great artists. Fully twenty of Landseer's finest works are in this collection.

The Jones collection is the richest room in the museum. It contains paintings, furniture, sculpture, bronzes, enamelled miniatures, and many curiosities of historical interest, all bequeathed to the museum by Mr. Jones, of Piccadilly, eight years ago.

The Dyce collection consists of oil paintings, miniatures, engravings, valuable manuscripts, and a costly library, all bequeathed to the museum by the eminent Shakespeare scholar whose name the room bears.

The Forster collection is the gift of Forster, the biographer of Dickens. It contains the original MSS. of nearly all of the novels of Dickens. This room is very rich in valuable autographs and manuscripts. An antique chair and desk, once the property of Oliver Goldsmith, are deposited here. I have in my note-book, many interesting quotations from manuscript letters exposed to view in the Forster Room, but I fear that I should weary my readers if I were to prolong this chapter.

On leaving this famous Museum, I felt that I had attempted to see altogether too much in a few hours. If it is little short of mockery to try to see so much in so short a time, how futile it is to try to convey to others an adequate conception of the contents of this vast repository of human art.

VIII.

LONDON LIFE.

"Dim miles of smoke behind—I look before,
　Through looming curtains of November rain,
　Till eyes and ears are weary with the strain;
Amid the glare and gloom, I hear the roar
Of life's sea, beating on a barren shore.
　Terrible arbiter of joy and pain !
　A thousand hopes are wrecks of thy disdain ;
A thousand hearts have learnt to love no more.
Over thy gleaming bridges on the street
　That ebbs and flows beneath the silent dome,
Life's pulse is throbbing at a fever heat.
　City of cities—battle-field and home
Of England's greatest, greatly wear their spoils,
Thou front and emblem of an Empire's toils."

London is a microcosm,—a little world of itself, and that not only on account of its size but also because everything is in it. Representatives of every nationality are congregated here. Here thrive all the varied extremes of human existence. Here flourish all arts and sciences and industries and professions. Here stand side by side gorgeous palaces and lofty temples, filthy hovels and sinks of iniquity.

No man knows London. Many who have lived in it all their lives know least of it. Behind many a counter and in many a workshop are "hands" whose fathers and grandfathers have paced the same oaken floors and worked at the same tasks as these toilers who will soon make way for a new generation. These hereditary slaves of labor know less of London than the visitor of a week. But how little knows the flitting visitor who has time to see only a few of the public places of interest and to run over a dozen of the principal streets. Not even the cabmen of the great city know it all, although their business every day takes them on a tour of exploration. To describe, therefore, the various phases of life in this interminable and labyrinthine London would be a task of a lifetime ; nay rather, to use a hyperbole from scripture, " if they should be written every one, I suppose that even the world itself could not contain the books that should be written." All that can be done, then, by one who has been able to take but a hasty and partial view of London life is to refer to a few salient features.

RICH AND POOR.

The very first thing that strikes the stranger as he takes his first stroll along the Strand and Fleet Street is the appalling fact that hundreds of his fellow creatures are in desperate need of a penny ! The ragged raiment and the pinched faces and the imploring looks and voices tell of the life-and-death struggle in progress here in the very centre of the world's civilization. When this revelation of degradation and woe has been fully realized, you impatiently exclaim, " How in the name of humanity can such social disorders prevail in this city of light and leading ?' The problem presses on you for solution and political economy closes your mouth with this grim reply : As the laws of progressive civilization find their highest expression in London, so do the laws of political science which necessarily throw into the hands of the rich the power of making customs and laws, and thus the rich must grow richer and the poor poorer and we must here expect to find men divided into the widest extremes of social condition—fabulous wealth and incredible penury :—in economics as in ethics to him that hath shall be given, and from him that hath not shall be taken even that which he hath. Whether this is true political economy or the inexorable logic of human selfishness will soon be determined, it is hoped. But if there is fault on the side of the rich, there is folly on the side of the poor. With moth-like fatuity the poor of England,— yes, of all Britain—fly from every side to the glare and glamour of the great city,—fly to scorching and to death. Those without friends and help in every quarter of the Kingdom are drawn by a strange and irresistible fascination to where humanity is gathered and packed in crowds, and once in the company of misery they have not the will to tear themselves away. And so it happens that grinding oppression and deluded subserviency join hand in hand to perpetuate a social condition which is deplorable and disgraceful.

Can no human prevision lift the poor of London to a higher plane? Are the blackamoors of Africa and the wild savages of southern seas to receive more sympathy and attention than the weary workers and the wandering waifs of London?

> " Day by day they rise and journey forth and wander
>   To the work-yard and the docks,
> Slouching sadly past the millionaires who squander
>   And the fatalist who mocks;
> And the women left behind them wear their fingers
>   To the sinews and the bone,
> Working sadly, whilst November daylight lingers,
>   Not for bread, but for a stone;
> And the ragged children huddled near their mothers,
>   Keep on starving in their cry.
> Thus they live in tribulation, oh, my brothers,
>   Thus they mercifully die!
>
> Grope your way up rotten staircases, and find them
>   By the dozen in a room;
> 'Tis but love and blind affection that can bind them
>   To this wretchedness and gloom.
> See the mother round the dying cinders crooning,
>   See the father in despair.
> See the daughter in consumption—she is swooning
>   From the foulness of the air.
> Hear the coughing and the crying and the groaning,
>   With the bare boards for a bed,
> Get the heartache with their miserable moaning,
>   'Give us bread! oh, give us bread!'"

And cannot the wisdom and wealth of humanity answer that reasonable cry? In a thousand garners there is food in abundance and to spare. What bold spirit will open the doors and let the poor flock in, and the mouths of the dying be filled?

STREET LIFE.

What inexhaustible food for meditation do London streets afford? What countless roads and alleys and lanes and courts, and every one with its distinctive characteristics? The narrow limits of this chapter will allow me to refer only to two types of streets,—such a crowded thoroughfare as the Strand, and such alleys as those that lead into Drury Lane.

If you take a position on the West Strand just where it enters Charing Cross at about five o'clock of a July afternoon you will see in half an hour enough for a week's reflections. Westward the main stream of traffic now flows. There rushes the well-dressed merchant to catch the 'bus that is to carry him homeward. Past you file a dozen men with placards on their backs announcing the attractions of some play or the bill-of-fare of some popular restaurant. The newsboy shouts in musical cadence the names of the papers on his arm. The match-seller torments you until you give him a penny to have him march on. The flower-girl with her wilting bouquets approaches you in a tone dreadfully pathetic and her ragged shawl and bonnetless head appeal successfully for two-pence. On flows the never-ending stream of pedestrians. All conditions and varieties of humanity surge along, every individual member of the jostling throng careful for himself but ignorant of and careless of all others. But it is time to move on yourself when the policemen begin to regard you with suspicion because you stand and gaze.

By way of contrast suppose you look into such quarters of poverty as abound in the swarming alleys off Drury Lane. "Shoals of children of all ages (I quote from a recent magazine article) encumbering th road-way, careless of carriage wheels, for no vehicle ever enters here except the huckster's cart or the parish hearse; frowsy, sodden, beer-soaked faces of women thrust out at the windows, cursing their brats who cry out in the dirt below; sauntering men who look at you, if you are decently dressed, as if your personal safety were a wrong and injustice to them; young girls, filthy, slatternly, leering, jeering, and ogling, imagination can readily conceive what for. Men do not grow to manhood in such slums and sunless ways, or women to virtue or dignity. All is squalor and filth and utter degradation of the divine image."

If one wishes to get picturesque views of London streets and street-life let him mount the spiral staircase at the back of an omnibus and take a seat on the top of the vehicle. How fresh the air up there and how exhilarating the prospect! You are lifted up above the pressing claims of beggars and hucksters and out of the pushing crowd and the risks of pedestrians. You are free to gaze without interruption, and the rattling pace of the horses raises your spirits to a sense of actual pleasure. At first you are rather nervous at the apparent recklessness with which your driver whisks you past the vehicles he meets, an interval of only an inch or two saving you from collision. But you soon put full confidence in the wonderful skill of these London drivers. Perhaps the most enjoyable ride one can have in an omnibus is from the centre of London to one of the suburbs and back again after nightfall when the streets are brilliantly lighted and the pavements are crowded. The perspective of Oxford Street or Piccadilly is very impressive. The two rows of shining lamps

"Stretch on and on before the sight,
Till the long vista endless seems."

THE PARKS.

The Parks have been called "The Lungs of London." Hyde Park, Regent's Park, Victoria Park, Battersea Park, St. James' Park, Green Park, together cover over 1600 acres right in the midst of the great city. To these parks flock every day thousands and thousands of women, children, and old men, to enjoy an hour in the fresh air away from the din and dust and smoke.

Regent's Park, the largest of the metropolitan parks, will serve as a type of all. Its artificial lake, its extensive flower gardens, its green shrubberies, its natural undulations, make it a resort of unsurpassed beauty. Visiting it at ten o'clock on the morning of Aug. 1st, I saw an animated scene. Rowers were moving over the lake in their light boats, snow-white swans swimming away from them as they passed. Crowds of joyous boys were playing cricket or throwing ball on every side. Well-dressed little girls were trundling hoops under the eyes of their nurses. Promenaders with easy gait went up and down the broad walk. Loiterers innumerable reclined on grassy slopes or sat on chairs and benches drinking in with keen gusto the sweet, pure air. Amid all this satisfying liveliness and beauty, however, were some distracting elements to which I could not close my eyes. The prevailing animation had its disagreeable contrast in snoring debauchees and wretched women from whose haggard faces had long since vanished the bloom of health and the happy glow of innocence.

THE CHURCHES.

I have already spoken of the two most famous of London churches, St. Paul's Cathedral and Westminster Abbey, but not as places of public worship. To them was I drawn not by preacher's voice, nor holy hymns, nor pealing organ. I wish now to speak of two London churches from a different point of view,—that of a listener to an earnest pulpit message.

On Sunday morning, July 27th, I made my way to Newington Butts to hear Spurgeon. I was ushered to a good seat in full view of the famous preacher. Six thousand weary souls followed the reading of the chapter and were thrilled by the waves of multitudinous song. When the speaker arose and announced his theme,—"Will a man rob God?"—I knew by the sternness of his face and the rasping fierceness of his voice that I had come to the wrong place in my loneliness for the gospel of hope and good cheer. For nearly an hour the doctrine of fire-and-brimstone vengeance was thundered forth in stentorian tones with all the vividness and vigor of eighteenth-century bigotry. The listening thousands were awed into a sort of acquiescence, as crowds usually are, by the very boldness and brilliancy of the orator. I saw the secret of the man's wonderful power, but I lamented the opportunity he had lost. What words of comfort in that hour he could have spoken! To how many wounded hearts he could have applied a blessed balm! With what an inspiration for toil and effort he could have sent away that vast congregation! As it was, they came for nourishing bread and he gave them a cold, hard stone.

I visited a week later another church, called, I think, "Bloomsbury Chapel." There I heard a sermon of a very different character. The preacher was a man whom I had learned to respect and admire on account of his ripe scholarship; henceforth I shall love him on account of his humanity. Stopford Brooke cannot draw as many hundreds as Spurgeon does thousands, for his discourses are in advance of the age and breathe the mellow spirit of the twentieth century. The sermon of that happy Sabbath I shall ever remember with grateful satisfaction. It was based on the passage describing the triumph of Moses over Pharaoh. With full, rich voice, in prophetic tones of marvellous power, he foretold in happy confidence the certain overthrow of all the Pharaohs of these modern days,—the political Pharaohs, the social Pharaohs, the ecclesiastical Pharaohs, the Pharaohs of false and tyrannical ideas in every sphere of human thought. As I listened to the splendid peroration of that earnest ambassador of God and saw his handsome face lit up with supernal glory, I wished that the oppressed myriads of groaning London could have heard that hopeful gospel, and I saw with clearer vision the slowly approaching millenium of our race.

HOME LIFE.

I had intended in this chapter to introduce my readers to several varieties of London homes, but I have already taxed their attention to the verge of weariness. I cannot, however, dismiss this subject without adverting to one happy home in the northwest of London into which I gained entrance by being provided with the "open sesame" of a friend's kind letter of introduction. The evening of Sunday, Aug. 3rd, will not soon fade from my memories of old London. Those three hours of home in a foreign land had a fragrance and an unction not here to be described. I see the happy faces gathered about the supper-table which has been placed on the green lawn in the rear of the house. I hear the prayers and hymns of praise which later in the evening ascend to heaven from the family worshipping in the cosy parlor. I cherish the last expressions on the faces of six interesting children as they one by one go off to their Sabbath-night rest. I had seen so much woe and misery in the week preceding and had been so worn with the din and clatter of the roaring streets that the quiet of suburban "Woodstock" was a solace and nepenthe. I had been long enough away from my own western home far over the sea to value keenly the warm hospitality of this snug English home.

IX.

STRATFORD-ON-AVON.

After ten days of sight-seeing in London I began to long for a sight of fresh fields and for a whiff of country air. I knew of one country town in England whose rural charms are enhanced by the traditions that cluster about an illustrious name,—a town to which for nearly three centuries have flocked pilgrims from every quarter of the globe. With much buoyancy of spirits, therefore, I stepped into the railway-coach at Paddington Station, in the afternoon of Aug. 5th, for a three-hours' ride to the birth-place of the immortal Shakespeare.

A succession of happy circumstances conspired to make my visit to Stratford one of unalloyed pleasure. I was glad to exchange the monotonous and interminable din of London for Arcadian peace, and the distressing sights of the city's want and woe for the abundance and comfort of a pastoral retreat. The day I had chosen for my visit to the literary Mecca of the world was an ideal English day, with mellow sunlight and balmy air. All the glories of midsummer were at their height, and more and more beautiful grew the landscapes as the train sped past old Oxford towards the central county of

> "This sceptred isle,
> This earth of majesty, this seat of Mars,
> This other Eden, demi-paradise."

The very passengers in the railway-coach after we left Warwick seemed under the influence of some subtle spell and were as silent as mummies. My fancy that they were thinking of Shakespeare was soon dispelled by their leaving the coach, one by one, before the train reached Stratford, and I was left to wonder whether any of them had ever read a play of Shakespeare. To tell the truth, I was glad to be left alone to my reflections as I approached the birth-place of the " Bard of Avon." Alone I rode in the 'bus to the "Shakespeare " and was ushered to a room over whose portal I read the word " Cymbeline," every room in the hotel having a Shakespearean name. Alone, after a delicious supper in the home-like hostelry, I took a stroll into the country.

It was "a beauteous evening, calm and free." What a place for dreamers and lotus-eaters are the environs of this neat Warwickshire town at eventide in August! These tidy footpaths and clean highways,—these trim hawthorn hedges,—these ancient elms and drooping chestnuts,—these lazy kine and silent sheep,—these meadows yellow with ripening corn or richly green with lush inviting grass,—this sleeping and noiseless river with its hallowed associations,—yon distant town with its gray old church,—the overarching sky with a brilliancy and depth of hue suggestive of what one reads of Italy,—the broad sun setting in celestial tranquillity,—all combine to form a natural picture of such transcendent loveliness that one can appreciate the rapturous swan-song of the dying Gaunt in which he styles England a "demi-paradise."

As I returned from an hour's saunter into the country and wandered through the meadows on the bank of the Avon opposite the ancient church where lie the mortal remains of "gentle Shakespeare," I was overcome by a mood quite unlike anything which any other spot on earth had ever engendered. I was affected by a novel combination of strange influences,—by the golden glow of the summer gloaming, by the magic of poetry that lighted up the landscape with the hues of the rainbow,—by the overmastering personality of the greatest mind that the fertile soil of Britain has produced. As I strolled along by 'Avon's pensive stream,' looking again and again towards the little church where the poet lies buried, I felt with exultation the full force of those appreciative lines written by young Milton only fourteen years after Shakespeare's death:

> "What needs my Shakespeare for his honored bones
> The labor of an age in piled stones?
> Or that his hallowed reliques should be hid
> Under a star-ypointing pyramid?
> Dear son of Memory! great heir of Fame!
> What need'st thou such weak virtues of thy name?
> Thou in our wonder and astonishment,
> Hast built thyself a live-long monument."

As I returned from the meadows to the town I could not fail to hear the piping of birds with unfamiliar notes, to see the graceful swans idly floating down the stream, to notice the picturesque reflections of grassy banks and ivied walls on the still surface of the lucid river. Crossing the fine old stone bridge of fourteen arches built in the time of Henry VII. I passed the ancient hostelry of the Red Horse which Washington Irving has made for ever famous. My evening walk I now felt had put me in touch with the spirit of the place, and I was fittingly prepared to visit on the morrow the many centres of interest in the town and vicinity.

Stratford is a small town of only 8000 inhabitants. It has nothing in it of importance but the places that are associated with the name of the great dramatist. Stratford is Shakespeare and Shakespeare is Stratford. Here the great poet was born and educated : here he passed much of his early life and his later years : here he died and was buried. Everywhere here, then, one sees and hears and feels Shakespeare. There is no distraction as in London with its thousand points of interest. Here every street has some tradition to tell of Shakespeare,—every ancient building recalls some epoch or incident in his chequered career. As you visit one place of note after another, beginning with his birthplace and ending with the church where he lies in dust, you feel more and more a unity of interest and impression quite dramatic.

Shakespeare's birthplace stands on Henley St. not far from the market. The old building has been restored more than once and so has not a very antique appearance, on the outside at least. After you enter the house, however, your thoughts are quickly carried back to remote days by the quaintness of everything you see. The plain old kitchen with its heavily timbered ceiling, its broken stone floor, and its wide open fire-place, soon surrounds you with the associations of three centuries ago. Over this rough floor the infant poet has toddled and romped. Here first

"Imperfect words, with childish trips,
Half unpronounced, slid through his infant lips."

By this desolate hearth, once warm with blazing logs and encircled by happy faces, Mary Arden used to sing to her open-eyed boy soft snatches of Warwickshire ballads or tell him ghostly tales of fascinating folklore.

The visitor is next conducted to the room up-stairs where Shakespeare was born. As you enter the room you notice the low ceiling, kept at one end from falling by iron supports,—the massive timber framework at the sides grown smooth and lustrous with time,—the long low window opposite the door,—the open fire-place,—the rough old floor of oak. You cannot fail to see, too, over the fire-place and on every inch of plaster the names, in pencil, of all sorts and conditions of men; but the old lady who guides you through will allow no more indiscriminate scribbling.

In a room across the hall—you need to bend your head to enter the low doorway—is kept in a fire-proof case the celebrated "Stratford portrait" of Shakespeare. From six o'clock in the evening until nine o'clock in the morning the heavy iron doors of the little room are closed securely to save from all chances of destruction this invaluable picture.

Before leaving the building you are directed to a room that serves as a Museum and Library where are collected many odds and ends of antiquarian interest. There is the hacked and dilapidated desk from the Grammar School over which the future dramatist acquired his "little Latin and less Greek." There is the signboard of the old Falcon Inn. There are many portraits of the poet, and many early editions of his works.

One cannot leave the old birthplace and walk down Henley Street and thence down High Street towards the old Grammar School without recalling the poet's own description of

> "The whining school-boy, with his satchel
> And shining morning face creeping like snail
> Unwillingly to school."

But perhaps the boy-poet was never of this type. Another English bard has pictured the youthful Shakespeare stretching forth his little arms to the mighty mother of poesy as she hands him the symbols of his art:

> "This pencil take (she said), whose colors clear
> Richly paint the vernal year:
> Thine too these golden Keys, immortal Boy!
> This can unlock the gates of Joy;
> Of Horror that and thrilling Fears,
> Or ope the sacred source of sympathetic tears."

One of my pleasantest memories of Stratford will ever be my forenoon walk across the fields, a mile or so through a characteristic bit of English rustic scenery, to the hamlet of Shottery and Anne Hathaway's cottage where the poet courted and won his beautiful wife and where he lived with her until he went up to London. Peaceful is Stratford, but serenely quiet is this beautiful rural spot. The cottage is very old and remains almost as it must have appeared in the days of Shakespeare. Like so many British cottages it is quite long and roofed with thatch. Pretty vines and blossoms cover the walls. Elm and walnut trees stand behind the cottage. At one side is an old-fashioned flower-garden from which I was privileged to bring away, by the grace of the lady in charge, a sprig of sweet jessamine and another of lavender whose faded yellow and blue-gray blooms lie before me as I write.

The room of chief interest in the cottage is the old parlour. It is a wonderful place with its old floor, old walls, old windows, old furniture, old everything. Not a modern touch interferes with the snug antiquity of the old room which breathes from every corner a placid breath from the sixteenth century. By yonder chimney-place, without a doubt, and on yonder settle of decaying oak, sat in the dear old days the most notable sweethearts of English literary history. Is there, in fact, any other building in the world around which hover from the distant past so many fragrant odors of love and courtship ? This antique thatch-covered country cottage has been an enduring love-lyric to twelve generations of English youths and maidens.

Making my way back to the town I passed the Guild Chapel, built in the reign of Henry VII. by the same Sir Hugh Clopton who erected the old bridge over the river. The bell of the old chapel still rings the curfew in summer at ten o'clock. Opposite to the Chapel is New Place, the house to which Shakespeare returned from London in 1597, and where he died in 1616.

Passing down Church Street and through Old Town I visited last of all the beautiful church of the Holy Trinity. I inspected the parish register and saw the entry recording the baptism of Shakespeare on the 26th of April, 1564, presumably three days after his birth. I must not attempt a description of the many interesting things in this old Gothic church,—as old in many parts as the fourteenth century. To visitors the chancel, of course, is the most interesting part of the church. Here are the grave and monumental bust of Shakespeare. The bust, which is life-size, is painted in natural colors, the hair and beard auburn and the eyes hazel. The doublet, or coat, is scarlet, and is covered with a loose, seamless black gown. This bust was placed here within seven years after the poet's death and for over two hundred and fifty years this face of stone has gazed day by day on curious pilgrims—an innumerable train from every land.

The following is the inscription beneath the bust:

IVDICIO PYLIVM GENIO SOCRATEM ARTE MARONEM
TERRA TEGIT POPVLVS MAERET OLYMPVS HABET.

(A free translation of this Latin couplet would be: "In judgment a Nestor; in genius a Socrates; in poetic art a Virgil. The earth covers him; the people mourn him; Heaven possesses him.")

Then comes the well-known stanza which may be thus modernized :

> " Stay, passenger, why goest thou by so fast?
> Read if thou canst, whom envious death hath placed
> Within this monument, Shakespeare with whom
> Quick nature died : whose name doth deck his tomb
> Far more than cost : since all that he hath writ,
> Leaves living art but page to serve his wit."

At a few feet from the wall, just below the monument, is the flat slab bearing the well-known malediction :—

GOOD FREND FOR IESVS SAKE FORBEARE

TO DIGG THE DVST ENCLOASED HEARE ;

BLESE BE ^E_Y MAN ^T_Y SPARES THES STONES,

AND CVRST BE HE ^T_Y MOVES MY BONES.

But for this imprecation the remains of the world's greatest poet would probably long ago have been removed from these quiet vaults to a corner of honor in Westminster Abbey. Thanks for once to the superstitions and prejudices of human nature that have religiously guarded these sacred ashes as a precious treasure and have retained them in the beautiful loneliness of this reverend church in this fine old English town.

X.

OXFORD AND CAMBRIDGE.

> " Ye sacred Nurseries of blooming Youth !
> In whose collegiate shelter England's Flowers
> Expand, enjoying through their vernal hours
> The air of liberty, the light of truth ;
> Much have ye suffered from Time's gnawing tooth ;
> Yet, O ye spires of Oxford ! domes and towers !
> Gardens and groves ! your presence overpowers
> The soberness of reason, till, in sooth,
> Transformed, and rushing on a bold exchange,
> I slight my own beloved Cam, to range
> Where silver Isis leads my stripling feet ;
> Pace the long avenue, or glide adown
> The stream-like windings of that glorious street—
> An eager Novice robed in fluttering gown ! "
>   —WORDSWORTH.

My visits to the "sacred Nurseries" of England's "blooming youth" were very brief,—scarcely long enough to justify me in attempting a description of these collegiate towns or in comparing their natural and architectural beauties and their educational advantages. The impressions that I did receive made me incline to Cambridge, notwithstanding the apostate preference of Wordsworth for the city on the "silver Isis."

OXFORD.

Oxford is one of the oldest cities in the world. So high an authority as Rawlinson attributes its foundation to a British king who lived a thousand years before the Christian era. At the time of Arthur there certainly existed here a flourishing Druidical school, and the place has been a famous seat of learning for over a thousand years.

More than once in English history has Oxford been a place of national importance. The city was besieged and taken by William the Conqueror. Here was signed the compact that gave the crown of England to the House of Plantagenet. Here met at various crises in the nation's history the Parliament of the realm, beginning with the "Mad Parliament" of Henry III. and ending with the Parliament summoned in 1681 by Charles II.—destined to be his last. Here were burned at the stake Cranmer, Ridley and Latimer. This is the city that during the great civil war loyally afforded a shelter to Charles I. and was the very centre and stronghold of monarchical principles. This is the city, too, that, goaded by the tyranny of James, welcomed the Prince of Orange with flying banners and blaring trumpets and general acclamations.

My visit to Oxford on August 7th was a veritable "flying visit." I had only a few hours to see some of the principal streets and to visit two of the colleges.

The finest street in Oxford is High Street. One may go even further and say that it is the finest street in England, and one of the most beautiful thoroughfares in Europe. This magnificent street has thus been described by an appreciative writer: "High Street is Oxford's pride,—a place which never fails to surprise the stranger with its beauty, and for which no amount of intimacy ever lessens our estimation. Had it been designed merely with a view to the general effect the result could not have been better. The great and rich variety of buildings—colleges and churches mingling with modern shops and old-fashioned dwellings—and the diversity of the styles in which they are constructed, are brought, by the gentle curvature of the street, into combination and contrast in the most pleasing manner. Nothing can well surpass the way in which the splendid architectural array opens gradually upon the passenger who descends it from Magdalen Bridge. Well may the poet celebrate 'The stream-like windings of that glorious street.' It is a noble street, and its general proportions are such as most favorably exhibit the magnificence of its edifices. It is of sufficient breadth to preserve an air of dignity, without being so wide as to cause the stately structures on either side to appear dwarfed; while the easy curvature brings the varied architectural forms and styles into opposition, and prevents anything like formality."

Oxford is a city of colleges. There are twenty-one colleges in all, scattered over the city, but no one of them a mile away from any other. Many of these colleges are known, at least by name, to every reader of English history and English literature, for out of these halls of learning have come many of the greatest men in English politics and English letters. Who has not heard of Baliol and Merton and Magdalen and Brasenose and St. John's and Pembroke?

Visitors to the colleges will soon discover that they have free access to all the college Quadrangles, and that they may enter the precincts of the buildings without any fear that they are trespassing. Entrance to the chapels and dining-halls may also be obtained on application to the porter and the payment of a small gratuity.

The first college that I visited was Christ Church, very near the Town Hall and Post Office. This college was founded by Cardinal Wolsey in 1525. I shall make no attempt to describe the massive grandeur of this ancient building. My recollections of Christ Church College are almost entirely connected with a half-hour's visit to its spacious and imposing dining-hall. The most interesting feature of this hall is the noble collection of paintings of college worthies that adorn the walls. All the distinguished graduates and students of this college, from its foundation to the present, gaze down from colored canvas upon you. There is the portrait of John Locke,—the most illustrious graduate of the olden times ; and there is the picture of one of whom this college is justly proud,—the most famous, perhaps, of modern orators and statesmen,— William Ewart Gladstone.

On inquiring for the oldest college in Oxford I was directed to University College on High Street which is said to have been founded by King Alfred in 872. When the porter found that I was a traveller from Canada he made inquiries about Goldwin Smith who, he said, had lectured in this College. He pointed out to me the two windows of the room occupied by the poet Shelley, who was expelled from the college at the age of seventeen for publishing a small treatise, "The Necessity of Atheism."

On entering the little chapel of University College I was startled by seeing on a marble tablet my own surname, to which was prefixed the unfamiliar praenomen,—Nathan. When I discovered that the letters (S. T. P.) appended to the name meant,—Professor of Sacred Theology, and learned from the Latin inscription on the stone slab that the departed had been *magister vigilantissimus* (a most zealous teacher) in the college for more than forty-three years, I could see no urgent reasons for claiming relationship with one who was probably no nearer of kin than thousands of the sons and daughters of Adam who possess such familiar names as Jones and Brown and Smith.

CAMBRIDGE.

Late in the afternoon of August 8th I found myself in Cambridge at "The Bull," a well equipped hotel right among the colleges. The hotel was almost empty and the city was very quiet. In term time 3,000 undergraduates throng the colleges and streets, but in the month of August the place goes to sleep and dreams. Very few gownsmen are to be seen, and the trades-folk, in the absence of their usual customers, are not strikingly active.

Cambridge has a population about equal to that of Oxford (40,000). The history of Cambridge, like that of Oxford, is lost in an obscure past; but as a famous place of study the town was not known abroad before the thirteenth century. What has been said about the number and location of the colleges of Oxford will apply almost without any change to those of Cambridge; they are about twenty in number and are clustered together within the limits of a square mile.

The names of the principal colleges of Cambridge are familiar to all scholars. The foremost college, of course, of the two University towns is Trinity College, Cambridge, with its 700 undergraduates, its brilliant record of achievements, and its commanding influence. It boasts of more celebrities of one kind and another than any other college in the world, a few of its illustrious names being Bacon, Herbert, Cowley, Dryden, Newton, Byron, Macaulay and Tennyson.

My recollections of Cambridge are mainly associated with a solitary evening ramble and a morning walk. I set out about seven o'clock in the evening to thread the labyrinths of the line of colleges near my hotel. I found it extremely difficult to keep my bearings, as many of the streets wind with the curves of the river Cam that flows through the city. Passing down the beautiful street called "King's Parade," I entered the great gate of King's College, and going through the court reached the rear of the noble cluster of buildings. The college courts and grounds in Cambridge are open to the public every day till dusk, and a visitor may pass in and out unchallenged provided he does not smoke, nor walk on the grass, nor take a dog for company.

Crossing the pretty bridge over the Cam behind King's College you enter a spacious and very beautiful park called "The Backs," because it runs behind the five colleges, Queen's, King's, Clare, Trinity, and St. John's, whose gigantic piles of ancient stone extend along the eastern bank of the river for nearly a mile. Running through this lovely park are many green, cool promenades, and everywhere through the stately trees and the verdant shrubs you catch glimpses of the fine old buildings and the placid river with its antique bridges. As I sat on a rustic seat beneath one of the ancient trees on that calm summer evening and thought of the many generations of men of might and light that had strolled through these scenes of matchless beauty and had drunk deep draughts of inspiration as they rested and meditated here, I felt that in a very real sense the spirits of departed intellect and genius haunt still these favored spots and confer on every succeeding generation of English youths the glorious birthright of their undying influence.

My morning walk of August 9th led me to the oldest and to the newest college in Cambridge. Peterhouse is the most ancient among the collegiate foundations of Cambridge, and indeed some parts of the present structure date back 600 years. No visitor should fail to see the beautiful chapel of Peterhouse with its richly carved interior and its very remarkable windows. It was to this college that the poet Gray belonged and from here, it will be remembered, he was driven by the pranks of his fellow-collegians and a sensitive disposition.

The newest college in Cambridge is Newnham,—the college for women. This college consists of three blocks of buildings in the south-west corner of the city,—Old Hall opened under the care of Miss Clough, a sister of the poet, in 1875,—Sidgwick Hall, named after Professor Sidgwick, the first promoter of the Cambridge Lectures for women,—and Clough Hall, named after the late Principal of Newnham. Miss Clough was connected with the College from its inception, and even before the opening of Old Hall she took charge of a house in Cambridge, having originally under her care only five students. To her the girls of England owe a deep debt of thanks for having first dared

> " To leap the rotten pales of prejudice,
> Disyoke their necks from custom, and assert
> None lordlier than themselves."

The vision of the Poet Laureate in " The Princess," stripped of its fine fancies, is being realized in these halls of Newnham, and in Girton, another college for women just out of Cambridge. The strict statutes of the visionary college of the poet—

> " Not for three years to correspond with home,
> Not for three years to cross the liberties,
> Not for three years to speak with any men "—

have no place, it is true, in the arrangements of Newnham and Girton. Not only do the fair students speak with the men on proper occasions, but since the University of Cambridge in 1881 opened its Tripos and

Previous Examinations to them, they have met the men on equal terms in the examinations of the University and have opened the eyes of England to the fact that Heaven has not put one sex under the ban of mental disabilities. When on the 7th of June, 1890, in the Senate House of Cambridge University the name of Philippa Garrett Fawcett, of Newnham College, was read out in the Class List of the mathematical Tripos, prefaced by the words "above the Senior Wrangler," the death-blow was finally given to the long-lived notion that intellectual limitations make woman the lesser man.

XI.

TENNYSON LAND.

My last few days in England were devoted mainly to a single object. I had visited the homes and haunts of three departed poets,—of Burns, of Scott, and of Shakespeare. To a living bard, the greatest of the present century, if not the sweetest singer of all times, I directed my attention for three short days, as a fitting conclusion of my happy summer rambles.

My visit to the land of Tennyson was in many respects my most delightful experience in Britain. It was a sort of exploration. Of this region the guide-books tell you not a word, and hither the great army of tourists have not yet begun to march. In visiting the other three centres of literary interest my enjoyment had often been lessened and my reflections had often been deadened by blatant voices and vulgar comments. On this three days' jaunt through Tennyson Land not one tourist crossed my path, and only twice did I hear the great name uttered. This interesting district, through all its woods and hills and streams and fields, its lonely roads and rustic hamlets, its windy beaches and prospects of blue sea, will be invaded, before the century ends, by pilgrims from many lands. I owe it to the interesting book of Mr. Walters that I have enjoyed the rare privilege of viewing these poetic haunts in the lifetime of the poet, and before the traces of the poet's footsteps have been profaned by the noisy multitude. It was this volume on the Land of Tennyson that kindled my interest in Lincolnshire scenes and turned my gaze in that direction. This book was my *vade-mecum* during my three days' excursion, and to it I shall have recourse more than once in the writing of these closing chapters.

LINCOLN.

Leaving Cambridge on Saturday, the 9th of August, I proceeded by way of Ely to Lincoln. As the train drew near the ancient city the triple-towered cathedral loomed up in massive boldness. This cathedral, one of the very finest in England, crowns the summit of a steep hill and overlooks the straggling, narrow streets. My wearisome ascent of the long, crooked street that leads to the cathedral was rewarded by an architectural view more impressive than any I had ever before seen. If the exterior of the magnificent church is grand beyond description, what shall I say of the wonders and mysteries of the awful interior? Neither pen sketch nor picture can produce a tithe of the reverence and awe that seize the beholder on entering this majestic temple. Lincoln cathedral was probably the first church of note that Tennyson ever saw, and thus did the sight fire his poetic impulses :

"Give me to wander at midnight alone,
Through some august cathedral, where, from high,

> The cold clear moon on the mosaic stone
> Comes glancing in gay colors gloriously,
> Through windows rich with glorious blazonry,
> Gilding the niches dim, where, side by side,
> Stand antique mitred prelates, whose bones lie
> Beneath the pavement, where their deeds of pride
> Were graven, but long since are worn away
> By constant feet of ages day by day."

I have been asked to compare the Lincoln cathedral with the famous York Minster which I stopped to see on my homeward journey through York. A comparison of the two churches is almost impossible as they differ so widely in the style of architecture,—that of Lincoln being composite with a leaning towards Early English,—that of York being one of the finest specimens in the world of pure Gothic. There is nothing in Lincoln cathedral, however, quite equal to the gorgeous eastern window in York Minster. This window is 75 feet high, 32 feet broad, and contains over 200 compartments, each a yard square, on which are depicted in exquisite and flaming designs as many scriptural subjects.

My visit to these two splendid churches of York and Lincoln greatly increased my respect and admiration for the artistic genius and consummate taste of our English forefathers. There were indeed giants in the days when these massive structures were erected. And what sublime faith and patience were exhibited in the slow construction of these mountains of polished stone! And how honest and substantial the work of those ancient toilers! The sculptured flowers and the emblazoned windows three-score feet above the pavement are as finely finished as if on a level with the eye of the beholder. The stones of the gigantic walls are everywhere fitted so nicely together that the eye can with difficulty discern the line of junction.

Lincoln has many other attractions besides its fine cathedral, but I neglected them all to prosecute my special pursuit. I have now brought my readers to the outskirts of Tennyson land. Let us enter the interesting region.

LOUTH.

Louth is a small town between Lincoln and the sea. When Tennyson was a boy the Grammar School at Louth was the principal educational institution in the county, and at this school in turn seven sons of Dr. Tennyson, Rector of Somersby, were pupils,—Frederick, Charles, Alfred, Edward, Horatio, Arthur, and Septimus. Alfred entered the school at Christmas, 1816, and remained for four years. The precocity of the young poet was remarkable, as he had completed the Grammar School course at the early age of eleven. The old Grammar School was torn down in 1869, and nothing remains about the new building to remind you of the past except a battered relic placed in the porch, —a begrimed old statue of King Edward VI., who is said to have founded the school.

Little is known of Tennyson's life in Louth. Only one of his school-fellows survives, and he reports that Alfred and Charles were inseparable companions but decidedly exclusive with respect to the other pupils.

The boys were grave beyond their years, but not otherwise remarkable.

The visitor to Louth cannot fail to admire the beautiful church where the Rev. Stephen Fytche, the father of Tennyson's mother, was vicar for many years. He died in 1799, and he and his wife are buried in the churchyard.

Another place I visited in Louth besides the Grammar School and the church. Opposite School House Lane is situated Westgate Place, a neat old house which will always be noted as one of the early homes of Tennyson. Here he lived four years with his aunt while attending school near by. Here later on he often spent weeks and perhaps months visiting his younger brothers. Here without a doubt his poetic emotion first took shape in juvenile verse. As I walked down the narrow stone-paved alley adjoining Westgate Place, and stood on the bridge crossing the tiny river Lud, and looked to the church just over the way, I thought of the noble-featured lad who had many a time and oft stood on that very spot, his young heart throbbing with glorious dreams of literary fame.

MABLETHORPE.

Where is Mablethorpe ? And what gives it fame ? It is a seaside hamlet east of Louth, but as regards fame its star has not yet risen. It is a place scarcely known out of Lincolnshire, and even the inhabitants of the little village, with a few exceptions, do not dream that within fifty years pilgrimages will be made to this sequestered spot by students of literature from every land. It was at Mablethorpe that young Tennyson obtained his first view of the sea. Here are "the sandy tracts, and the hollow ocean-ridges roaring into cataracts" that we read of in "Locksley Hall." Here about the beach the poet wandered "nourishing a youth sublime with the fairy tales of science, and the long result of Time." In Mablethorpe sixty years ago the Tennyson family were accustomed to spend the summer months, and all the sea-pictures that abound in the early poems of Tennyson take their form and color from this Lincolnshire coast.

I reached Mablethorpe, by train from Louth, at seven o'clock on Saturday night, and found quarters for the Sunday at an inn bearing the odd name of "Book-in-Hand." Perhaps the name was given in anticipation of my visit, for whenever I left the hotel I carried in my hand the white-and-gilt manual already mentioned. After supper I roamed on the beautiful and spacious beach for over two hours. As far as the eye could see in both directions stretched the wide belt of sand. The tide was going out and a few children were toying with the receding waters and picking up the pale pink shells and rushing in glad abandon hither and thither, the evening breezes playing with their dishevelled hair. How Tennyson loved to wander along this free strand in the rare days of youth's sweet dreams! How many varying aspects of these Norland waters, in calm and in storm, under the bright flash of day or beneath the shimmering moonlight, has he seen with the clear eyes of the rapt worshipper of Nature and drawn with the delicate pencil of unrivalled genius.

Sunday, August 10th, was a day of cloud and wind and rain, but I was glad to have it so, as there had been a monotony of fair weather for three full weeks. Although the sky lowered ominously I set out after breakfast to walk along the beach to Sutton-on-the-Sea,—a summer resort about three miles south of Mablethorpe. An hour brought me to my destination, but as the tide had turned and a thick mist was sweeping up, I thought it prudent to retrace my steps. My prudence proved to be imprudence. I had not gone a mile before the situation became alarmingly interesting. The North-easter roared among the sea-caves. The sea-foam flew far landward over dune and wold. The tide plunged and roared in its shoreward march. I was driven for shelter behind "the heaped hills that mound the sea." The thick grey mist turned imperceptibly to rain. My umbrella was of no service in the fierce wind. I fled for refuge into one of Nature's inns until the sudden tempest had spent its fury. Shortly after noon I reached my hotel, not much the worse for my exhilarating adventure. I shall hereafter appreciate Tennyson's numerous references to such storms,

" When to land
Bluster the winds and tides the self-same way,
Crisp foam-flakes scud along the level sand,
Torn from the fringe of spray."

On Sunday afternoon from the window of my room I saw in the distance a pretty white house which seemed to be the very one that shone in gilt on the cover of my Tennyson manual. After making my way to the quaint old cottage and questioning a ruddy Lincolnshire lass who stood at the door, I found that my identification was correct. I saw before me the "lowly cottage" referred to by the poet in his "Ode to Memory"—

> "Whence we see
> Stretched wide and wild the waste enormous marsh,
> Where from the frequent bridge,
> Like emblems of infinity,
> The trenched waters run from sky to sky."

Leaving the curious, long, low-roofed house where were composed many of the Poet Laureate's finest verses of sea and shore, and crossing "the trenched waters" by a tiny bridge, I wandered over the moist beach and the rugged dunes till again driven in by mist and rain.

All readers of Tennyson know that many of his later poems are tinged with gloomy hues. The glories and the wonders of the world in which he spent his youth and early manhood have taken to themselves wings, and nature now is bleak and bare. No longer does he see bright visions and hear wondrous voices, but what he sees and hears is as it is. This difference is nowhere more clearly marked than in these lines descriptive of two contrasted views of the old beach at Mablethorpe :

> "Here often when a child, I lay reclined,
> I took delight in this locality,

Here stood the infant Ilion of the mind,
And here the Grecian ships did seem to be.
And here again I come, and only find
The drain-cut levels of the marshy lea—
Gray sandbanks and pale sunsets,—dreary wind,
Dim shores, dense rains, and heavy-clouded sea!"

XII.

TENNYSON LAND—CONCLUSION.

In this concluding chapter I shall give a brief account of my visit to the birthplace of the Poet Laureate. I need not recount my difficulties in discovering the whereabouts of Somersby and the mode of access to it. I need not tell how near I came to visiting by mistake a place called Somerby, a village some leagues away from the one I was seeking. As quickly as may be I shall take my readers to the little parish among the wolds which Tennyson has made immortal,—

> " The well-beloved place
> Where first he gazed upon the sky."

HORNCASTLE.

From Mablethorpe I returned to Lincoln on August 11th, and thence took train for Horncastle, a market town "in the circle of the hills" about 20 miles east. On my arrival in Horncastle I found the place crowded with visitors, and I was greeted with stares and smiles when I acknowledged that I had never heard of the famous Horncastle horse-fair, the largest in Lincolnshire, and at one time the largest in Britain. I soon found, to my cost, that the fair had drawn many dealers from long distances, for the accommodation of every hotel in the town was taxed to the utmost limit, and I was obliged to ask the genial proprietor of "The Bull" to secure me lodgings in a private house.

Horncastle is only two leagues distant from Tennyson's early home, and it was the market town to which some members of the Tennyson family frequently came to replenish the domestic larder. Many a time, in the early years of the century, did young Tennyson walk from his home to Horncastle, and it would be impossible even for himself to tell how largely these walks, solitary or not, have affected the thought and tinged the complexion of his poetic description of natural scenery.

In another very real way Horncastle has touched the life of Tennyson. After he had become the most noted poet in Britain,—in the very year, in fact, in which he was appointed as Poet Laureate,—at the age of forty-one, he married Emily Sellwood, the daughter of a Horncastle lawyer, and the niece of Sir John Franklin (born at the neighboring village of Spilsby). Emily Sellwood, now Lady Tennyson, has had her memory embalmed in more than one of her husbands's poems. She is the "Edith" of "Locksley Hall Sixty Years After." To her he wrote from Edinburgh the poem, "The Daisy," beginning

"O Love, what hours were thine and mine,
In lands of palm and southern pine."

She is also honored in that sweet dedication

> " Dear, near, and true—no truer Time himself
> Can prove you, tho' he make you evermore
> Dearer and nearer."

SOMERSBY.

Tuesday, August 12th, was to me a day of exquisite enjoyment. I set out alone in the morning from Horncastle to make my way on foot to Somersby, Tennyson's birthplace, six miles north-east. In the early part of my walk I met many farmers bringing in their fine-looking horses to be sold to foreign buyers and carried to all parts of England and the continent. I caught many a phrase from the passers-by that reminded me of the quaint dialect of "The Northern Farmer." These farmers were all, I take it, animated by the spirit of the farmer of the poem :

> " Dosn't thou 'ear my 'erse's legs, as they canters awaay ?
> Proputty, proputty, proputty—that's what I 'ears 'em saay."

Of all the passengers on the Horncastle road that day I alone was intent, not on the value of horses, but on the charms of poetry and of poetic associations.

The road to Somersby is extremely rural ; rural in a thoroughly English sense. It winds and turns and twists between the bordering hawthorn hedges,—some trim and neat, some wild and shaggy. At every bend of the road the landscape varies. Here a cosy cottage ; there a picturesque windmill : here a wide stretch of pasture covered with thick-fleeced sheep ; there a distant hill wrapt in blue-grey mist : here a group of laborers cutting the ripe corn ; there a quiet woodland slope where grow the poet's trees in rich variety, the ash, the elm, the lime, the oak.

The many curves and turns in the road make it very difficult for the stranger to keep the right course. The finger-posts to be seen at every corner and cross-way are indispensable. I was forcibly struck with the fact that Somersby is a very insignificant place when at one cross-way I found the finger-boards filled with names, but could find no Somersby there. In my perplexity I sat down and copied out the curious names on the boards which pointed in four directions:

	Belchford.	Fulletby.	
Tointon			Salmonby
Horncastle			Tetford
	Spilsby.	Greetham	

I decided to follow the Tetford road which after a little distance bent almost backward towards Horncastle, but which ultimately proved to be the right route for Somersby.

What a silent land I found as I approached the end of my journey ! In the last three miles I saw only two persons. The only creatures in sight were hundreds on hundreds of sheep and cattle.

Now Somersby is near at hand. The road turns down a steep incline and passes through a shady arbor. The branches of the trees that skirt the narrow way meet overhead and cast their tremulous shadows at your feet. All is quiet but the faint rustling of the leaves, or the distant clamor of the daws and rooks. You feel that you have reached an actual lotus-land,— an enchanted realm. No longer does it seem strange that Tennyson composed while walking along this Lincolnshire road the loveliest of his sea-lyrics, "Break, break, break."

But it is no surge of the sea that is now heard in the distance. There is no mistaking that musical tinkling. Yonder is the bridge under which flows the brook with its haunting sound of rippling waters that " come from haunts of coot and hern." The witchery of the brook's refrain, I hear it still :

> " I chatter over stony ways,
>   In little sharps and trebles,
> I bubble into eddying bays,
>   I babble on the pebbles.
>
> I steal by lawns and grassy plots,
>   I slide by hazel covers ;
> I move the sweet forget-me-nots
>   That grow for happy lovers.

> I slip, I slide, I gloom, I glance,
>   Among my skimming swallows;
> I make the netted sunbeam dance
>   Against my sandy shallows.
>
> I murmur under moon and stars
>   In brambly wildernesses;
> I linger by my shingly bars;
>   I loiter round my cresses.
>
> I chatter, chatter, as I flow
>   To join the brimming river,
> For men may come and men may go,
>   But I go on for ever."

There is not such another brook in the world as "Somersby Beck." Had it not found its way into the poetry of words its inimitable voice would still arrest the attention of the traveller, but the magic melody of the poet's words have hallowed the sweet beck and heightened its attractiveness, and though men may come and men may go the melodious brook will go on for ever singing through the sweet meadows of the poet's song. I am afraid to tell how long I sat on the grassy bank listening to the wonderful music of the gleeful rivulet. Nor will I own how often since that August day I have come again under the irresistible spell of the brook.

Almost within sound of the brook is the hamlet of Somersby, inhabited by two-score simple old-world people. And yonder on the right is the pretty white house where the Laureate was born. It is a curious tile-covered house, cosily situated in an ideal environment. It nestles among the trees, and before it is a beautiful lawn separated from the public road by the holly hedge planted by old Dr. Tennyson when the poet was a child. The house was the Rectory of the parish for nearly a hundred years, but the present rector, Rev. John Soper, has deserted the historic house and dwells in the neighboring parish.

And this is the house where Tennyson spent his youthful prime and where he composed many of his chief works. As "In Memoriam" is the record of a soul struggle fought out on this very ground, we may expect to find in that poem many local references. To this place often came Arthur Hallam " from brawling courts and dusty purlieus of the law " to drink the cooler air and mark " the landscape winking through the heat." Here often he joined the rector's happy family " in dance and song and game and jest." To this place was brought the cruel news of Hallam's death which felled the poet's sister in a swoon and turned her orange-flowers to cypress. Here for many gloomy years the broken-hearted poet plied the " sad mechanic exercise " of writing verse to soothe his restless heart and brain.

The only other structure of interest in Somersby i the little church of which Tennyson's father was rector for many years. It is very small and very old. To the right of the porch is an ancient cross of the fourteenth century, bearing figures of the Virgin and the Crucifixion. Over the porch is a dial with the motto, "Time passeth," and the date 1751. The interior of the church is uninviting. The rough pews would seat about forty worshippers ; the pulpit in the corner is small and mean ; the windows that pierce the walls at irregular distances have been made at various times and are of different shapes and sizes. The "cold baptismal font" in the rear calls up such dismal memories of the past that the visitor is glad to escape from the clammy, sickly air.

In a conspicuous place in front of the church is seen the tombstone erected over the grave of Dr. Tennyson. The epitaph runs as follows :

TO THE MEMORY

OF

THE REV. GEO. CLAYTON TENNYSON, LL. D.,

ELDEST SON OF GEORGE TENNYSON, ESQ.,

RECTOR OF THIS PARISH,

WHO

DEPARTED THIS LIFE

ON THE

16TH DAY OF MARCH, 1831.

AGED 52 YEARS.

When, a few years after the father's death, the Tennysons departed from Somersby "to live within the stranger's land" we hear a minor chord in the great memorial elegy sounding thus :

> " Our father's dust is left alone
> And silent under other snows :
> There in due time the woodbine blows,
> The violet comes, but we are gone."

About a furlong beyond Somersby Church is one of the prettiest spots this dull old earth can show,— "Holywell Glen" :

> " Here are cool mosses deep,
> And through the moss the ivies creep,
> And in the stream the long-leaved flowers weep,
> And from the craggy ledge the poppy hangs in sleep."

It is a wild, romantic spot,—the favorite haunt, we may be sure, of the poet's boyhood. Trees of many kinds—larch and spruce and ash and beech and sycamore—clothe the steep sides of a natural terrace that slopes down to the bottom of a gorge through which flows a limpid stream. This beautiful glen takes its name from a natural well over which the stream courses. Long years ago, it is said, visitors came from far and near to taste of this "holy well" and to enjoy its healing virtues. If the water of this well has no supernatural merits, I can at least attest its superior quality, taking a draught of it, as I did, in my extremity of thirst on a warm August afternoon.

I had always clung to the ancient saying that poets are born, not made. My views are somewhat altered since I have seen the glories of Holywell Glen and all the enchantments of rustic Somersby. Here, if anywhere, Nature could inspire the most sluggish spirit and put some music into the tamest heart.

But I must leave this rustic nook and this quiet hamlet. As I leave Somersby behind and climb the hill on the road to Horncastle I recall those sad stanzas of "In Memoriam" in which Tennyson gives voice to his regret at leaving forever the home and the haunts of his young days:

> " I climb the hill; from end to end
> Of all the landscape underneath,

I find no place that does not breathe
Some gracious memory ot my friend.

No gray old grange, nor lonely fold,
   Or low morass and whispering reed,
   Or simple stile from mead to mead,
Or sheepwalk up the windy wold ;

Nor heavy knoll of ash and haw
   That hears the latest linnet trill,
   Nor quarry trench'd along the hill,
And haunted by the wrangling daw ;

Nor runlet trickling from the rock ;
   Nor pastoral rivulet that swerves
   To left and right thro' meadowy curves,
That feed the mothers of the flock ;

But each has pleased a kindred eye,
   And each reflects a kindlier day ;
   And, leaving these, to pass away,
1 think once more he seems to die."

www.ingramcontent.com/pod-product-compliance
Lightning Source LLC
Chambersburg PA
CBHW021918180426
43199CB00032B/692